Education and Language Restoration

CONTEMPORARY NATIVE AMERICAN ISSUES

·◇·◇·◇·

Education and Language Restoration

Jon Allan Reyhner
Professor of Education, Northern Arizona University

Foreword by
Walter Echo-Hawk
Senior Staff Attorney, Native American Rights Fund

Introduction by
Paul Rosier
Assistant Professor of History, Villanova University

CHELSEA HOUSE
PUBLISHERS
A Haights Cross Communications Company ®
Philadelphia

T 31942

L

CHELSEA HOUSE PUBLISHERS

VP, NEW PRODUCT DEVELOPMENT Sally Cheney
DIRECTOR OF PRODUCTION Kim Shinners
CREATIVE MANAGER Takeshi Takahashi
MANUFACTURING MANAGER Diann Grasse

Staff for EDUCATION AND LANGUAGE RESTORATION

EXECUTIVE EDITOR Lee Marcott
EDITOR Christian Green
PRODUCTION EDITOR Noelle Nardone
PHOTO EDITOR Sarah Bloom
SERIES AND COVER DESIGNER Takeshi Takahashi
LAYOUT EJB Publishing Services

Library of Congress Cataloging-in-Publication Data
Reyhner, Jon Allan.
  Education and language restoration / Jon Reyhner.
    p. cm. — (Contemporary Native American issues)
  Includes bibliographical references and index.
  ISBN 0-7910-7970-8
  1. Indians of North America—Education (Higher) 2. Indians of North America—
Cultural assimilation. 3. Indians of North America—Languages—Revival. 4. Indians
of North America—Languages—Study and teaching. 5. Multicultural education—
United States. 6. Education, Bilingual—United States. 7. Indian universities and col-
leges—Government policy—United States. I. Title. II. Series.
  E97.R49 2004
  306.44'973'08997073—dc22
                              2004003267

Contents

Foreword

Walter Echo-Hawk

N ative Americans share common aspirations, and a history and fate with indigenous people around the world. International law defines indigenous peoples as non-European populations who resided in lands colonized by Europeans before the colonists arrived. The United Nations estimates that approximately 300 million persons worldwide are variously known as tribal, Native, aboriginal, or indigenous. From 1492 to 1945, European nations competed to conquer, colonize, and Christianize the rest of the world. Indigenous peoples faced a difficult, life-altering experience, because colonization invariably meant the invasion of their homelands, appropriation of their lands, destruction of their habitats and ways of life, and sometimes genocide.

Though colonialism was repudiated and most colonies achieved independence, the circumstances of indigenous peoples has not improved in countries where newly independent nations adopted the preexisting colonial system for dealing with indigenous peoples. In such nations, colonial patterns still exist. The paramount challenge to human rights in these nations, including our own, is to find just ways to protect the human, political, cultural, and property rights of their indigenous people.

Contemporary issues, including those of culture, can be understood against the backdrop of colonialism and the closely related need to strengthen laws to protect indigenous rights. For example, colonists invariably retained close cultural ties to their distant homelands and rarely adopted their indigenous neighbors' values, cultures, or ways of looking at Mother Earth. Instead, they imposed their cultures, languages, and religions upon tribal people through the use of missionaries, schools, soldiers, and governments.

In the mid-1800s, U.S. government policymakers used the "Vanishing Red Man" theory, which was advanced by anthropologists at the time, as justification for the forcible removal of Native American tribes and for taking their lands. The policy did not work; America's indigenous peoples did not "vanish" as predicted. Native American tribes are still here despite suffering great difficulties since the arrival of Europeans, including an enormous loss of life and land brought on by disease, warfare, and genocide. Nonetheless, diverse groups survived, thrived, and continue to be an important part of American society.

Today, Native Americans depend on domestic law to protect their remaining cultural integrity but often that law is weak and ill-suited for the task, and sometimes does not exist at all. For example, U.S. federal law fails to protect indigenous holy places, even though other nations throughout the world take on the responsibility of protecting sacred sites within their borders. Congress is aware of this loophole in religious liberty but does not remedy it. Other laws promote assimilation, like the "English only" laws that infringe upon the right of Native Americans to retain their indigenous languages.

Another example concerns indigenous property rights. The *very* purpose of colonialism was to provide riches, property, and resources for European coffers. To that end, a massive one-way transfer of property from indigenous to nonindigenous hands occurred in most colonies. This included land, natural resources, and personal property (called *artifacts* by anthropologists). Even dead bodies (called *specimens* or *archaeological resources* by anthropologists) were dug up and carried away. The appropriation has been extended to intellectual property: aboriginal plant and animal knowledge patented by corporations; tribal names, art, and symbols converted into trademarks; and religious beliefs and practices *borrowed* by members of the New Age movement. Even tribal identities have been taken by "wannabes" masquerading as Native Americans for personal, professional, or commercial gain. In beleaguered Native eyes, little else is left to take. Native legal efforts attempt to stem and reverse this one-way transfer of property and protect what little remains.

Through it all, Native American tribes have played an important role in the American political system. The U.S. Constitution describes the political relationships among the federal government, states, Native American tribes, and foreign nations. Hundreds of tribal governments comprise our political system as "domestic dependent nations." They exercise power over Native American reservations, provide for their tribal citizens, engage in economic development, and sometimes come into conflict with states over intergovernmental disputes. Many tribes own and manage vast tracts of tribal land, extensive water rights, and other natural resources. The United States holds legal title to this property in trust. As trustee, the United States exercises significant power over the lives of Native Americans and their communities; and it is responsible for their well-being. These "nations within nations" are not found on international maps and are invisible to many in our own country.

Prior to 1900, about five hundred treaties between Native American tribes and the United States were duly ratified by the Senate and signed into law by the president. Treaties contain hard-fought agreements that were earned on American battlefields and made between Native American tribes and the United States. They opened vast expanses of Native American land to white settlement, protected remaining Native property, and created the political relationships with the U.S. government that remain to this day. As President George H.W. Bush said during his inaugural address in 1989, "great nations like great men must keep their word." Though many treaties were broken, many promises are honored by the United States today and upheld by federal courts.

The history, heritage, and aspirations of Native Americans create many challenges today. Concern for tribal sovereignty, self-determination, and cultural survival are familiar among Native Americans. Their struggles to protect treaty rights (such as hunting, fishing, and gathering rights), achieve freedom of religion, and protect Mother Earth (including land, resources, and habitat) are commonplace challenges, and sometimes include the task of repatriating dead relatives from museums. Each year, Congress passes laws affecting vital Native interests and the Supreme Court decides crucial cases. The hardships that Native Americans have endured to keep their identity are little known to many Americans. From the times of Red Cloud, Seattle, and Chief Joseph, Native leaders have fought to achieve these freedoms for their people. These ideals even today motivate many Native American soldiers to fight for our country in distant lands, like Iraq and Afghanistan, with the hope that the principles fought for abroad will be granted to their relatives at home.

Today, vibrant Native American communities make significant contributions to our rich national heritage. Evidence of this can be found in the recently opened National Museum of the American Indian, in Washington, D.C. It is also found throughout the pages of *Native Peoples* magazine and other Native media. It fills the best galleries, museums, and auction houses. It can be seen in the art, dance, music, philosophy, religion, literature, and film made by Native Americans, which rank among the world's finest. Visitors crowd tribal casinos and other enterprises that dot Native American reservations in growing numbers. Tribal governments, courts, and agencies are more sophisticated than ever before. Native American-controlled schools and colleges are restoring the importance of culture, traditions, and elders in education, and instill Native pride in students. The determination to retain indigenous cultures can be seen through the resurgence of tribal language, culture, and religious ceremonial life.

Yet many old problems persist. Too many Native Americans are impoverished and in poor health; living at the very bottom of almost all socioeconomic indicators and often in violence-ridden communities where disease, such as AIDS, knows no racial or cultural boundaries. Some socioeconomic problems stem from the aftermath of colonization of Native lands, peoples, and resources, or from efforts to stamp out Native culture and religion. Others stem from prejudice and hostility against Native people that has long characterized race relations in the United States.

As our nation matures, we must reject, once and for all, harmful policies and notions of assimilation and ethnocentrism, and embrace cultural relativism in our relations with the Native peoples who comprise our diverse society. History teaches where racial stereotypes, myths, and fictions prevail, human rights violations soon follow. But social change comes slowly and ethnocentrism remains deeply rooted in mass media and other corners of society. To little avail, Native people have told Hollywood to stop stereotyping Native Americans, protested against harmful racial stereotypes used by groups like the "Redskin" football team, and requested appropriate coverage of Native issues by the mainstream media. Native life is far different than how it has been depicted in the movies and by school and professional mascots.

Regrettably, schools do not teach us about Native Americans; textbooks largely ignore the subject. Sidebar information is provided only when Pilgrims or other American heroes are discussed, but Native Americans mostly "disappear" after dining with Pilgrims, leaving students to wonder about their fate. As a result, the people who met Columbus, Coronado, Custer, and Lewis and Clark are still here, but remain a mystery to legislators, policymakers, and judges who decide vital Native interests. Those interests are too often overlooked, marginalized, or subordinated by the rest of society. The widespread lack of education and information is the most serious problem confronting America's Native people today.

CONTEMPORARY NATIVE AMERICAN ISSUES will help remedy the information gap and enable youth to better understand the issues mentioned above. We are fortunate to have comprehensive data compiled in this series for students. Armed with facts, this generation can address Native American challenges justly.

Walter R. Echo-Hawk
Boulder, Colorado
March 2005

Introduction

Paul Rosier

During the mid-1970s, I attended Swarthmore High School in suburban Philadelphia, Pennsylvania. There, I learned little about Native Americans other than that they had lived in teepees, hunted buffalo, and faced great hardships in adapting to modern life at the end of the nineteenth century. But I learned nothing about Native Americans' experiences in the twentieth century. And as a member of the Tomahawks, the high school football team, I was constantly reminded that Native Americans had been violent and had used primitive weapons like tomahawks. Movies and television shows reinforced these notions in my young and impressionable mind.

It is my experience from teaching Native American history at the university level that students in middle and high schools across the country, have not, with some exceptions, learned much more about Native Americans in the twentieth century than I did thirty years ago. Several years ago, one of my students asked me if Native Americans still live in tepees. He and many others like him continue to be presented with a limited and biased interpretation of Native Americans, largely from popular culture, especially sports, where professional teams, such as the Washington Redskins, and mascots, such as the University of Illinois' Chief Illiniwek, continue to portray Native Americans as historical objects, not as citizens of this nation and as members of distinct tribal communities.

In 1990, President George H.W. Bush approved a joint resolution of Congress that designated November National Indian Heritage Month, and over the following years similar proclamations were made by presidents William J. Clinton and George W. Bush. On November 1, 1997, President Clinton stated: "As we enter the next millennium we have an exciting opportunity to open a new era of understanding, cooperation, and respect among all of America's people. We must work together to tear down the walls of separation and mistrust and build a strong foundation for the future." In November 2001, President Bush echoed Clinton by saying, "I call on all Americans to learn more about the history and heritage of the Native peoples of this great land. Such actions reaffirm our appreciation and respect for their traditions and way of life and can help to preserve an important part of our culture for generations yet to come."

We still have work to do to further "understanding, cooperation, and respect among all of America's people" and to "learn more about the history and heritage of the Native peoples of this great land." The information presented in CONTEMPORARY NATIVE AMERICAN ISSUES is designed to address the challenges set forth by presidents Clinton and Bush, and debunk the inaccurate perceptions of Native Americans that stretches back to our nation's founding and continues today. For example, schoolchildren's first intellectual exposure to Native Americans may well be through the Declaration of Independence, which describes Native Americans as "merciless Indian savages, whose known rule of warfare is an undistinguished destruction of all ages, sexes, and conditions."

The series' authors are scholars who have studied and written about the issues that affect today's Native Americans. Each scholar committed to write for this series because they share my belief that educating our youth about Native Americans should begin earlier in our schools and that the subject matter should be presented accurately.

Outside the classroom, young students' first visual exposure to Native Americans likely comes from sporting contests or in popular culture. First impressions matter. C. Richard King, Associate Professor of Comparative Ethnic Studies at Washington State University, discusses this important issue in his volume, *Media Images and Representations*. King looks at how these early impressions of Native Americans persist in film and television, journalism, sports mascots, indigenous media, and the internet. But he also looks at how Native Americans themselves have protested these images and tried to create new ones that more accurately reflect their history, heritage, and contemporary attitudes.

In *Education and Language Restoration*, Jon Allan Reyhner examines the history of how Native Americans have been educated in boarding schools or mission schools to become assimilated into mainstream American society. Reyhner, Professor of Education at Northern Arizona University, considers how Native Americans have recently created educational systems to give students the opportunity to learn about their culture and to revitalize dormant languages. Like non-Native American students, Native students should invest time and energy in learning about Native American culture and history.

This educational process is important to help Native Americans deal with a myriad of social problems that affects many communities in our country. In their volume *Social Life and Issues*, Roe Walker Bubar and Irene S. Vernon, professors at the Center for Applied Studies in American Ethnicity at Colorado State University, review the various social issues that Native Americans face, including health problems like AIDS and alcoholism. They also consider how Native American communities try to resolve these social and health crises by using traditional healing ceremonies and religious practices that are hundreds of years old.

One very important issue that has helped Native American communities heal is repatriation. Joe Edward Watkins, Associate Professor of Anthropology at the University of New Mexico, examines this significant matter in his volume, *Sacred Sites and Repatriation*. Repatriation involves the process of the government returning to individual tribes the remains of ancestors stolen from graves in the nineteenth century, as well as pots and ceremonial objects also taken from graves or stolen from reservations. Native Americans have fought for the return of objects and remains but also to protect sacred sites from being developed. Such places have religious or spiritual meaning and their protection is important to ensure continued practice of traditional ceremonies that allow Native Americans to address the social and health problems that Vernon and Bubar describe.

In *Political Issues*, Deborah Welch, the Director of the Public History Program and Associate Professor of History at Longwood University, writes about how Native Americans reclaimed political power and used it to strengthen their communities through legislation that promoted both repatriation and the protection of sacred sites, as well as their ability to practice their religion and traditions, which the federal government had prohibited into the 1970s. Native American tribal communities have fought for their sovereignty for decades. Sovereignty means that tribal governments set the rules and regulations for living within reservation boundaries. Federally recognized tribal groups maintain their own courts to prosecute crimes—with the exception of major crimes, that is, rape, arson, and murder. Native Americans living on their own reservations generally do not need to obey state regulations pertaining to hunting and fishing and do not pay state income or excise taxes, though they are responsible for paying federal income taxes.

Tribal governments also help to create economic opportunities for their people, the subject of Deborah Welch's second volume, *Economic Issues and Development*. In this book, Welch examines the ways in which Native Americans have tried to create employment in businesses, which include ranching, mining, golf resorts, and casinos. She also considers how Native Americans have tried to develop projects within the context of their environmental traditions. As with other elements of their lives, Native Americans try to use their tribal histories and ceremonies to confront the economic challenges of modern life; to prosper by being *both* Native and American, while ensuring the health of Mother Earth.

Limited coverage of Native American life in schools, newspapers, and broadcast media has helped to perpetuate Americans' stereotypical views of Native Americans as either wealthy from gambling or suffering from poverty and alcoholism. The real picture is not so easy to paint and involves more than 550 separate Native American nations within the United States, which includes 4.1 million people who identify themselves as solely or in part Native American. The goal of this series is to explore the many different dimensions of the complex world of today's Native Americans, who are divided by geography, politics, traditions, goals, and even by what they want to be called, Native American or American Indian. Most Native Americans, however, prefer to be identified by their tribal name, for example, Lakota (Sioux), Blackfeet, or Diné (Navajo). And yet Native Americans are some of the most patriotic Americans, in part because their ancestors and relatives have died fighting in the name of freedom, a freedom that has allowed them to be both Native and American. As U.S. Army Sergeant Leonard Gouge of the Oklahoma Muscogee Creek community put it shortly after the September 11 attacks, "By supporting the American way of life, I am preserving the Indian way of life."

Paul Rosier
Villanova, Pennsylvania
March 2005

1

Assimilation and the Native American

European settlers colonizing the Americas after 1492 found the Native inhabitants to be very helpful about how to live in the New World. With its unique climates, plants, and wildlife, the Natives often lived in the most fertile areas that the colonists wanted for themselves. A debate raged early on, even reaching the pope in Rome, as to whether these Native inhabitants were human beings with rights to the lands they occupied, or whether they were somehow less than human and could be pushed aside, enslaved, or even done away with. All of these options were tried at least once in the past five hundred years. Sadly, some aspects of this inhumane debate are still with us today.

The hundreds of reservations in the United States and reserves in Canada that were set aside for Native Americans in the nineteenth century are still their homelands, but many Native Americans in the present day have left to look for opportunities elsewhere. They now

In the 1870s, the U.S. government began a policy of assimilating Native Americans, which led to the establishment of the Carlisle Industrial Indian School in 1879. Many Native American children, such as these Chiracahua Apaches, were forcibly taken from their families and transported across the country to Pennsylvania, where they were indoctrinated in the ways of Euro-American society.

live alongside descendants of the European settlers who over-ran most of their lands and the Native American way of life. To take advantage of this new non-Native American life, Native inhabitants in North America have had to learn English, while Native inhabitants in Central and South America have had to learn Spanish.

Back in the nineteenth century, Native Americans had to be Christian, speak a European language, and dress like Europeans to be considered human. The more liberal-minded European colonists sought to teach Native Americans their ways and set about converting them to Christianity, instructing them to speak English, Spanish, or French, and dressing them in "citizen" clothes. Native Americans were expected to forget their previous "savage" ways of thinking and to stop speaking their Native languages. This process of losing one's Native identity and speaking, acting, and dressing like someone else is called *assimilation*. Assimilation involves losing one's native or home culture and being forced to adopt a new culture. A *culture* is defined by the characteristics that a specific group of people share. It embraces their whole way of life, including their religion, language, clothing, music, and civic leadership.

The necessity to assimilate Native Americans and other minorities is based on the human characteristic of *ethnocentrism*. Experts who study cultures, *anthropologists*, coined the term ethnocentrism to describe how virtually every culture in the world tends to think that their own culture is superior to all other cultures, and that their way of doing things is normal and other ways of doing things are strange, abnormal, and inferior. Regarding religion, this type of thinking leads each culture to claim its religion as the one "true" religion. Because European immigrants viewed themselves as being at the pinnacle of civilization and Native Americans as "savages," they did not think they needed to learn anything about Native Americans and their cultures in order to teach them. Native American cultures and traditions were seen as impediments to progress and should be quickly left behind and forgotten.

This ethnocentrism is not of recent origin. The ancient Greeks thought anyone who did not share their culture was a "barbarian," and early Romans felt the same way even to the point of throwing Christians to the lions because they refused to worship Roman gods. When he started teaching on the Pine Ridge Reservation in South Dakota in 1899, Albert Kneale found the U.S. government's Indian Bureau "always went on the assumption that any Indian custom was, *per se*, objectionable, whereas the customs of whites were the ways of civilization."[1]

Most of the educational efforts applied to the Native

inhabitants of the Americas were driven by the notion of European superiority and Indian "savagery." At the beginning of the twentieth century, anthropologist Franz Boas researched Native American cultures and disputed the still-popular idea that Native American and other foreign cultures are inferior to Euro-American cultures. Boas developed the concept of *cultural relativism* that says that cultures are not better or worse than one another; they are just different.

The ethnocentric rejection of Native American customs as "savage" was done without any thorough examination of these cultures. President Franklin D. Roosevelt's Commissioner of Indian Affairs, John Collier, declared that modern society has lost the "passion and reverence for human personality and for the web of life and the earth which the American Indians have tended as a central sacred fire."[2] He concluded in his memoirs that

> *Assimilation*, not into our culture but into modern life, and *preservation* and *intensification of heritage* are not hostile choices, excluding one another, but are interdependent through and through. . . . It is the ancient tribal, village, communal organization which must conquer the modern world.[3]

Native American and other ethnic minority students continue to face assimilationist pressures in U.S. and Canadian schools because of the ethnocentric belief that mainstream American culture is superior to other cultures and the English language is superior to other languages.

A HISTORY OF ASSIMILATION

To accomplish the goal of assimilating Native Americans in colonial times, Christian missionaries sought to gather the more nomadic Native Americans into settled villages and to put their children into schools. When Native American parents and grandparents resisted having their children transformed into "white people," missionaries and government officials supported taking Native American children away from their families by force and putting them in boarding schools where they could be indoctrinated into European ways of thinking and speaking.

In 1819, the U.S. government started a Civilization Fund that provided $10,000 a year to Christian missionaries to educate Native Americans. Missionaries played a major role in running Indian schools until Protestant and Catholic missionaries started fighting over who should get the government's money. Because the Protestants thought the Catholics were getting too much money, the Protestants persuaded the government to directly handle the Indian schools in the 1890s, changing the administration of the Indian schools permanently. The United States had set up an Indian Office first in the War Department in 1824 and then in the Department of the Interior in 1849. The major role of this office in its early years was removing eastern Native Americans to Indian Territory (now Oklahoma)

Indigenous Values

At the 1996 annual meeting of the Alaska Association for Bilingual Education, I picked up a card describing Iñupiaq Eskimo values. On one side the card read "Every Iñupiaq is responsible to all other Inupiat for the survival of our cultural spirit, and the values and traditions through which it survives. Through our extended family, we retain, teach, and live our Iñupiaq way." The other side read, "With guidance and support from Elders, we must teach our children Iñupiaq values" and then it listed the values of "knowledge of language, sharing, respect for others, cooperation, respect for elders, love for children, hard work, knowledge of family tree, avoidance of conflict, respect for nature, spirituality, humor, family roles, hunter success, domestic skills, humility, [and] responsibility to tribe." The card concluded with "Our understanding of our universe and our place in it is a belief in God and a respect for all his creations." I find it hard to reject these values in favor of the values I see portrayed in most of today's popular television shows, movies, and music.

Shown here is a group of Chiracahua Apaches four months after their arrival at Carlisle in 1886. The founder of the military-style school, Richard Henry Pratt, followed a policy of "kill the Indian and save the man." Pratt believed in forcing Indians to learn English, while forbidding them to speak their own language.

or otherwise confining them on Native American reservations. As the Native Americans had their land taken away, the U.S. government promised in treaty after treaty to provide schools for their children so that they could learn and live in peace as farmers alongside white settlers. In these schools, students were kept apart from their parents for years at a time, taught Christianity, and punished for speaking their Native languages.

In the last quarter of the nineteenth century, the primary function of the Indian Office was to run these schools with the hope that once Native American children were educated they would quickly leave their tribal cultures and live alongside white Americans. The naïve optimism that Native Americans would quickly assimilate if they would just become Christians and speak English is brought to light through the words of the Indian Office's Superintendent of Indian Schools, John H. Oberly, who in 1885 optimistically predicted:

> [I]f there were a sufficient number of reservation boarding-school-buildings to accommodate all the Indian children of school age, and these buildings could be filled and kept filled with Indian pupils, the Indian problem would be solved within the school age of the Indian child now six years old.[4]

History has proved Oberly's prediction wrong, and more than a century later this so-called "Indian problem" has not been solved. Many Native Americans still insist on the freedom to retain their Native American identity, including their tribal affiliations, traditional religions, and languages. In 1947, the Indian Office was renamed the Bureau of Indian Affairs (BIA), and although most Native American children today attend public schools, the BIA still operates boarding and day schools and funds tribally operated schools, mostly on Native American reservations in the western United States.

Boarding Schools

Boarding schools were a major tool for educating Native American children in the United States and Canada well into the twentieth century, and a few remain in operation today. Unlike the elite boarding schools for children of the rich, Indian boarding schools were usually of very poor quality, and students received classroom instruction for only half the day and worked to maintain the school during the other half. The result was that most Indian boarding school graduates received less education than the children of non-Native Americans who attended public schools and received classroom instruction both morning and afternoon. With this substandard education, Native Americans were not prepared to compete for jobs with non-Native Americans.

The unfairness of expecting Native Americans to lead

successful lives with a second-class education did not go unnoticed by humanitarian reformers, and during the twentieth century efforts were made to improve the education of Native American children. However, non-Native Americans were not eager to pay more taxes to educate Native Americans. Improvements came slowly, and during World War II some previous advances were lost due to the lack of funding.

THE CIVIL RIGHTS MOVEMENT

The Civil Rights movement of the 1960s brought a renewed focus of attention on the second-class citizenship of all American minorities. In 1963, Martin Luther King spoke of

Negative Effects of Assimilationist Schooling

The effects of assimilationist schooling on Native Americans were described by Dillon Platero, the first director of the Navajos' Division of Education, in his 1975 description of "Kee":

Kee was sent to boarding school as a child where—as was the practice—he was punished for speaking Navajo. Since he was only allowed to return home during Christmas and summer, he lost contact with his family. Kee withdrew from both the White and Navajo worlds as he grew older because he could not comfortably communicate in either language. He became one of the many thousand Navajos who were nonlingual—a man without a language. By the time he was 16, Kee was an alcoholic, uneducated, and despondent—without identity.*

Platero declared that Kee's experiences were more the rule than the exception, and he emphasized the need to use the Navajo language more with Navajo students.

* Dillon Platero, "Bilingual Education in the Navajo Nation," in *Proceedings of the First Inter-American Conference on Bilingual Education*, eds. Rudolph C. Troike and Nancy Modiano, (Arlington, Va: Center for Applied Linguistics, 1975), 56–61.

having "a dream that my four little children will one day live in a nation where they will not be judged by the color of their skin but by the content of their character." That dream included his children and other children of color getting an education equal to that of white students. The Civil Rights movement intensified a long-standing desire of American Indian and Alaska Native peoples to have more control over their lives, lands, and the education of their children.

The increased interest in the quality of Native American education during the Civil Rights movement led to new studies. The government-sponsored National Study of Indian Education was carried out between 1967 and 1971. It involved visiting schools, testing students, and interviewing parents. Based on its findings, Estelle Fuchs and Robert J. Havighurst reported in 1972 in their book, *To Live on This Earth*, that although most Native American students and parents approved of their schools, Native American community leaders were "overwhelmingly in favor of the school doing something to help Native American students learn about their tribal culture" and that the most common parental suggestion was that "schools should pay more attention to the Indian heritage." They concluded from the study that

> With minor exceptions the history of Indian education had been primarily the transmission of white American education, little altered, to the Indian child as a one-way process. The institution of the school is one that was imposed by and controlled by the non-Indian society, its pedagogy and curriculum little changed for the Indian children, its goals primarily aimed at removing the child from his aboriginal culture and assimilating him into the dominant white culture. Whether coercive or persuasive, this assimilationist goal of schooling has been minimally effective with Indian children, as indicated by their record of absenteeism, retardation, and high dropout rates.[5]

The study found that most Native American students and parents approved of their schools, but that community leaders and parents wanted schools to teach students more about tribal culture. It also found that when given a nonverbal intelligence test, Native American children on average were slightly more intelligent than white students.

A Senate Special Subcommittee on Indian Education investigation, chaired first by Senator Robert Kennedy and after his assassination by his brother, Edward Kennedy, held hearings around the country and collected seven volumes of testimony. Its findings were summarized in the 1969 report, *Indian Education: A National Tragedy, a National Challenge,* also known as the Kennedy Report. The report was even more critical of schools serving Native American students than the National Study of Indian Education, and it echoed studies from a century before that assimilationist schooling was not particularly successful and could have very negative effects on Native American students. The subcommittee declared that:

1) Drop-out rates are twice the national average in both public and Federal schools. Some school districts have dropout rates approaching 100 percent.

2) Achievement levels of Indian children are 2 to 3 years below those of white students; and the Indian child falls progressively further behind the longer he stays in school.

3) Only 1 percent of Indian children in elementary schools have Indian teachers or principals.

4) One-fourth of elementary and secondary school teachers—by their own admission—would prefer not to teach Indian children; and Indian children, more than any other minority group, believe themselves to be "below average" in intelligence.[6]

Attorney Ralph Nader, who later ran for president as a Green Party candidate with Native American activist Winona LaDuke (Ojibwe) as his vice-presidential nominee, testified before the Special Subcommittee that

> In any school with Indian students, BIA or public, cultural conflict is inevitable. The student, bringing with him all the values, attitudes, and beliefs that constitute his "Indianness," is expected to subordinate that Indianness to the general American standards of the school. The fact that he, the student, must do all the modifying, all the compromising, seems to say something to him about the relative value of his own culture as opposed to that of the school. . . .
>
> It has been estimated that for half of the Indians enrolled in Federal schools English is not the first language learned. Yet, when the child enters school he is expected to function in a totally English-speaking environment. He muddles along in this educational void until he learns to assign meaning to the sounds the teacher makes. By the time he has begun to understand English, he has already fallen well behind in all the basic skill areas. In fact, it appears that his language handicap increases as he moves through school. And although it is no longer official BIA policy to discourage use of native languages, many reports in the hearings indicate the contrary in practice.[7]

Supported by civil rights activists of all colors, Native Americans pressed for more *self-determination*—which is the policy that Native Americans should make decisions for themselves—especially through their tribal governments, rather than having the federal government in Washington make decisions for them. In a special message to Congress in 1970, President Richard Nixon wrote:

> [T]he story of the Indian in America is something more than

In the early 1970s, President Richard Nixon named Louis Bruce (pictured here), one of the founders and executive director of the National Congress of American Indians, as commissioner of Indian affairs. Bruce grew up on St. Regis Reservation in New York and is of both Mohawk and Sioux heritage.

the record of the white man's frequent aggression, broken agreements, intermittent remorse and prolonged failure. It is a record also of endurance, of survival, of adaptation and creativity in the face of overwhelming obstacles. It is a record of enormous contributions to this country—to its art and culture, to its strength and spirit, to its sense of history and its sense of purpose.

It is long past time that the Indian policies of the Federal government began to recognize and build upon the capacities and insights of the Indian people. Both as a matter of justice and as a matter of enlightened social policy, we must begin to act on the basis of what the Indians themselves have long been telling us. The time has come to break decisively with the past and to create the conditions for a new era in which the Indian future is determined by Indian acts and Indian decisions.[8]

Nixon appointed Louis Bruce (Mohawk-Sioux), one of the founders and executive director of the National Congress of American Indians, as commissioner of Indian affairs. The first major victory of the new self-determination policy was the passage of the Indian Education Act in 1972. This act provided funds for programs for Native American children in public schools on and off Native American reservations, which are

Civil Rights Commission Report

Passing laws like the Civil Rights Act of 1964 and the Indian Education Act of 1972 did not mean the immediate end of discrimination. In 1973, the U.S. Commission on Civil Rights reported that in the southwestern United States, Indian school advisory committees lacked power, and the average Native American student was two to three years behind the typical white student. Joy Hanley, the Navajo Nation's Director of Elementary Education, testified that the public schools pretend they are teaching middle-class white children. In 1974, the Oklahoma Advisory Committee to the Commission expressed concerns about the negative view of Native Americans in textbooks and the disciplining of Native American boys for having long hair.

In 1975, the Civil Rights Commission reported that 70 percent of Navajo first graders did not have a first-grade-level command of English, that bilingual education was gaining Navajo support, and that there were only 188 Navajo teachers out of the 2,800 teachers on the Navajo Reservation. It found that new teachers were not adequately prepared to teach Native American students. In addition, Navajo parents were still being excluded from decision making. There were also no interpreters at some schools and Johnson-O'Malley Program (JOM) funds were being misused. Student witnesses from Gallup-McKinley High School in New Mexico voiced concerns about biased textbooks. The commission's report titled *The Navajo Nation: An American Colony* concluded that Navajo language and culture were largely ignored in schools. The report also noted that a Navajo teacher, my wife, was reprimanded by her school principal when she used her Navajo language to help explain the meaning of English words to her Navajo-speaking kindergarten students.

designed to solve some of the problems identified in the National Study of Indian Education and the Kennedy Report. All public schools with ten or more Native American students were eligible to receive funding for programs intended to meet the special needs of Native American students, including the use of culturally relevant and bilingual curriculum materials. Schools were required to involve Native American parents and communities in designing these programs. It also established an Office of Indian Education and a National Advisory Council on Indian Education.

Although the Civil Rights movement led to Native American students learning more about their Native American heritage in schools, mainstream assimilationist pressures persist today, doing battle with Native American efforts to revitalize their languages and cultures. School can still be considered by Native Americans and other minorities a place of becoming "white"; one in which they learn about the very world that Indians see as rejecting their Indianness.

American Indian Movement

Martin Luther King's nonviolent approach to change, patterned after the teachings of India's Mahatma Gandhi, was not shared by all members of America's oppressed minorities. The Civil Rights movement radicalized some minorities who saw no hope in following America's democratic political system, especially after more moderate leaders like King were assassinated or jailed. Some blacks, who unlike King, saw the democratic political system shut off from them, formed the Black Panthers. Hispanics created the Brown Berets. Native Americans of a similar mind joined the American Indian Movement (AIM) and threatened armed resistance to oppression. Other Native Americans staunchly supported existing institutions and saw the Civil Rights movement as a Communist effort to subvert America. Subsequently, they fought any attempts for change. The culmination of efforts by

AIM members to get the attention of Americans came with the 1973 armed takeover of the village of Wounded Knee on the Pine Ridge Reservation in South Dakota that lasted for seventy-one days. Pine Ridge became the center of conflict between supporters of AIM, who were allied with Lakota Indian traditionalists, and conservative supporters of the more assimilated and mixed-blood (part white) tribal government. Similar, but less violent conflicts played out in other Native American nations, which resulted in more attention being paid to the education of Native American children in public and BIA schools.

Virgil Kills Straight, an Oglala Sioux, wrote in the *Navajo Times* in July 1972 that "AIM was born out of the dark violence of police brutality and the voiceless despair of injustice in the courts of Minneapolis. . . . AIM is at first a spiritual movement, a religious rebirth, and then a rebirth of Indian dignity." AIM members reached out to Native American youth to get them involved in the movement for Native American rights. In the fall of 1972, Navajo students at Window Rock High School in Fort Defiance, Arizona, walked out to protest the student dress code (which did not allow girls to wear pants except on extremely cold days) and the lack of a Native American culture program. An additional issue was a football player who was not allowed to play because of his long hair. This walkout led to more Native Americans being elected to the school board and the hiring of a school superintendent and high school principal who were both Native American. In North Carolina in the spring of 1973, sixty-five Tuscaroras were arrested in a protest because AIM leader Vernon Bellecourt was not allowed to speak to high school students about Wounded Knee.

One common assimilationist practice in the years prior to the Civil Rights movement, which was opposed by AIM and other Native American leaders, was the suppression of Native American languages in mission, BIA, and public schools. Speaking Native languages was sometimes simply discouraged; although at other times students received a variety of punishments, including having one's mouth washed out with soap for speaking "Indian"; a punishment usually restricted to students who used swear words in non-Native American schools.

However, as repressive practices were eliminated and discipline loosened in BIA schools during the Civil Rights era, students occasionally failed to show the necessary responsibility that comes with more freedom. In the years that followed, alcohol abuse and absences from class increased, and a heightened level of disrespect was shown toward teachers. As a result, the quality of education in those schools went down. At the large Intermountain Boarding School in Brigham City, Utah, there was a three-day riot in 1975 that led to injured police officers and destroyed police cars. At Phoenix Indian School, alcohol abuse became epidemic in the 1980s and during the 1984–1985 school year, 256 of the 700 students enrolled were expelled. Both schools were later closed.

In 1975, the Indian Self-Determination and Education Assistance Act was passed, allowing elected Native American school boards to take over BIA schools. Many ethnic minority parents, including Native American parents, thought change was needed. Textbooks at the beginning of the Civil Rights era focused on a Euro-American point of view, and most of the people in the illustrations and stories were white. In the 1960s, not much had changed from 1908, when author George Wharton James reported how Native American students repeatedly complained to him about the American history they were forced to study:

> When we read in the United States history of white men fighting to defend their females, their homes, their corn-fields, their towns, and their hunting-grounds, they are always called "patriots," and the children are urged to follow the example of these brave, noble, and gallant men. But when Indians—our ancestors, even our own parents—have fought to defend us and our homes, corn-fields, and hunting-grounds they are called vindictive and merciless savages, bloody murderers, and everything else that is vile.[9]

2

Community-Controlled Schools and Tribal Colleges

In the United States, the government policy of Indian self-determination promoted more tribal self-government and led to the founding of Rough Rock Demonstration School (RRDS) on the Navajo Reservation. Martin Luther King's dream for his children began to take shape for Native American children when RRDS opened in 1966. Navajo Tribal Chairman Raymond Nakai described it as

> [T]he nation's most unique and exciting experiment in the field of Indian education. It is proving conclusively that Navajo parents do care and are able to provide both leadership and control over the education of their children. It is thrilling to witness the involvement of Navajo parents in all aspects of the school and its program. This is what we want for the Navajo people throughout the reservation.[10]

Navajo tribal leaders, local Rough Rock Navajo elders, and Dr. Robert Roessel, Jr., a professor at Arizona State University, teamed up to establish RRDS as the first Native American community-controlled school in modern times. It was an experimental project, a joint effort of President Lyndon Johnson's "War on Poverty" Office of Economic Opportunity (OEO) and the Bureau of Indian Affairs (BIA). Starting with 220 students, almost all staying in the dorms, its bold mission was, according to one observer, John Collier, Jr., to "correct a hundred years of Native American mis-education."[11]

Roessel, the school's first director, became interested in Native Americans while growing up in the Midwest. Soon after becoming a teacher on the Navajo Reservation, he married a Navajo. He felt that "Navahos should have a major role in determining the educational objectives and the educational program(s) for Navaho children" and criticized the fact that most schools with Indian students taught little or nothing about Indians.[12] Roessel saw the key features of RRDS as local control and "cultural identification." Rough Rock instituted a Navajo/English bilingual program that included teaching Navajo history. Roessel wrote in 1968 that the school promoted a "'both-and' approach to Indian Education—taking the best of the dominant culture and the best of the Indian culture and putting these together in the classroom so the child grows up with a positive sense of well-being, a positive self-image, with pride in his heritage."[13]

The promise of RRDS was to strengthen the identity of its Navajo students, to have Navajo parents take control of the education of their children, and to provide a quality education for Navajo children. For RRDS and other tribal-controlled schools this promise is still yet to be fully realized. Local control can be seen as a value *per se*, regardless of the quality of education that it shapes for indigenous students. Although the quality of education delivered prior to local control was nothing to be proud of, it can be argued that local control was offered as a cure-all and that it has failed to deliver the superior education that its advocates promised. Taxpayers supporting these schools are justified with their concerns about the way federal and state tax dollars are being spent to educate Native American students today.

RRDS became a media showcase that claimed to have fifteen thousand visitors in its first two years. Visitors included influential U.S. senators such as Robert and Edward Kennedy and Walter Mondale. One of Rough Rock's early achievements was the publication of Navajo curriculum materials for students to read, including *Black Mountain Boy*, *Coyote Stories*, *Rough Rock History*, *Grandfather Stories*, *Navaho Biographies*, and *Navaho History*.

Although Rough Rock received a good deal of favorable publicity, it also had its critics. University of Chicago professor Eric Erickson's 1969 evaluation of Rough Rock reported that it failed to develop a sound curriculum and teachers were given little support. Later studies reported high teacher turnover and student absenteeism. In the decades that followed, more and more BIA schools came under local control, but the problems associated with RRDS were often left unfixed. Schools continued to hire non-Native American teachers who knew nothing about Native Americans and relied on textbooks written for non-Native American students. Local Native Americans often had little experience with schooling and lacked understanding about the complexities of curriculum development and the administration of schools that are in many ways complicated businesses.

RRDS school board members were accused of hiring their relatives rather than the most qualified applicants, and the curriculum was described as chaotic. Reminiscent of the routines in the old BIA boarding schools, a student described Rough Rock's bell schedule:

In the morning a bell rings at 6:00 to get up. At 7:00 a bell rings for roll call and breakfast. At 8:30 a bell rings to get to school. At 11:30, a bell rings to go back to the dorm to get fixed for lunch. At 12:00 a bell rings for lunch (which) you get free and all the same thing. At 3:30 a bell rings to go to the dorm; at 6:00 one rings for dinner. At 9:00 all the girls go to bed.[14]

According to Erickson, the Navajo school board wanted rigorous attendance rules, but Roessel considered this contrary to Navajo beliefs. Erickson concluded that Roessel supported teaching traditional Navajo culture at the expense of preparing students to live in the modern world. Gloria Emerson, a Navajo who was a Harvard graduate student and OEO education specialist, visited RRDS in 1967 and 1968. In a 1970 article, she declared that Rough Rock was "bent on selling an image to whites, to Navajo communities, to bureaucrats, and, most important, to funding sources. I felt then that the discrepancies between the puff pieces and the reality at Rough Rock were probably due to administrative weaknesses." She described Rough Rock as an "'ego-tripping' showcase" and its administration as "chaotic." She felt it was demeaning to condone "administrative deficiencies" at Rough Rock as "Navajo 'cultural' ways."[15]

The local jobs provided by schools like RRDS on reservations with high unemployment can overshadow educational concerns. Because school jobs provided the major source of family income in the Rough Rock community, board members focused more of their attention on hiring and firing local people rather than on their school's educational program. The school board was often more interested in purchasing water troughs and hay for the community's sheep and the various OEO-funded saddle and moccasin making, silversmithing, and medicine man training than on the best way to teach reading, math, and science to their children.

Much of the effort made by school administrators at RRDS and other community-controlled schools was dedicated to trying to acquire funding, often requiring key administrators to spend a good deal of time away from the school in meetings with government and foundation officials in Washington, D.C., and elsewhere. For example, in April 1969, Dillon Platero, who replaced Roessel as the school's director in 1968, visited Salt Lake City, San Antonio, Albuquerque, Washington, D.C., and New York. Funding often arrived late, and federal grant money varied greatly from year to year. Ethelou Yazzie, Rough Rock's director after Dillon Platero went on to become the first director of his tribe's new Division of Education in 1973, wrote:

It is June:
The BIA contract is not signed. We have no idea what our budget for fall will be. No teacher is certain that his/her job will be funded. No money has yet arrived to fund the clinic, our arts and crafts co-op is locked. The curriculum center will stay open half-time because there is no money. There is no capital to produce its product, or to train apprentices in writing, editing, and printing. Our summer school is severely limited in its offerings and staff size, relying heavily on volunteers.
This is the way it is at Rough Rock. We expect a crisis a month, and we are never disappointed. . . .
The system is a monumental fake and hoax. It is a political game in which the community or school that refuses to lie down and not die wins just enough to stand up for the next punch.[16]

These problems, included late paychecks, led to a high annual turnover in teaching staff.

RRDS was a failure as a "Demonstration School" in the sense that other schools could not copy its programs, both because of its disorganized curriculum and the impossibility of providing other schools the extra money it initially received from the OEO. Roessel's emphasis on using athletics, especially

Throughout his life, former Navajo Tribal Chairman Peterson Zah, who is shown here during his inauguration in 1983, has been a proponent of teaching the history, culture, and language of his tribe in Navajo schools. Today, Zah serves as a special advisor to the president of Arizona State University, where he has been instrumental in helping to double the enrollment of Native Americans at the school.

basketball and rodeo, served a valuable purpose in securing parental support, and providing recreation for young Navajos, but it also helped develop a trend still seen in many Indian schools and communities in which athletics are valued more than academics. Another questionable trend that Rough Rock helped establish is the local school board prioritizing hiring relatives rather than discussing how and what students were being taught. Navajo tribal chairman Peterson Zah noted that community factionalism can be made worse by one group getting control of the school board. In a 1983 speech, Zah supported community control but warned that "Parents should vote against, and campaign against those candidates who are only interested in the income they receive as board members, or in handing out jobs to their relatives, political supporters, and friends." On the positive side, RRDS blazed a path for other Native American communities like Rock Point to follow in taking control of their schools.

ROCK POINT COMMUNITY SCHOOL

The community of Rock Point moved more gradually to local control of their school than their neighbors in Rough Rock. Wayne Holm, who like Roessel was a non-Navajo who had married a Navajo, started working at Rock Point in 1960 and first helped to improve the BIA school's English as a second language (ESL) program. Historically, students learning English in school were submersed in it and expected to catch up with native speakers of English as John Oberly had predicted in the nineteenth century. However, this usually did not happen and finally in 1974, the U.S. Supreme Court decided in the case *Lau v. Nichols* that non-English speaking students needed to be provided with special ESL teaching methods or be taught first in their Native language as they learned English.

As was the case for Native American students elsewhere, students at Rock Point had test scores far below the national average, because they were being taught and tested in a language that some were just learning. In fact in 1960, students at the isolated Rock Point School had the lowest test scores in the area. Holm argued in a 1964 *Journal of American Indian Education* article that "in *most* grade-level Bureau [BIA] classrooms American English, as a spoken language, is not taught. . . . Too many Navaho children struggle daily to read and comprehend a language—American English—which they neither speak nor 'hear' well."[17] The next year the BIA's Director of Education, Hildegard Thompson, wrote that Rock Point's efforts affirmed the basic principles of the BIA's ESL program. She called for teachers to ask themselves: "Am I relating my oral English

Maria Tsosie's About-Face on Bilingual Education

Daniel McLaughlin, who now works at Diné College, conducted a study of the Rock Point Community and its school. In that study he quotes "Maria Tsosie" who went to a summer program at Harvard University in Boston, Massachusetts. There she almost certainly experienced *culture shock*, which is the disruption people usually deal with when they move from one culture they are familiar with to another culture in which almost everything is strange. Upon returning from Harvard she declared:

> Before I left the reservation I was really for bilingual education. I had gone through it from first through twelfth grades, and I thought everybody here needed it. I didn't think people should lose their language. That's why I thought bilingual education was viable. Everybody should know their own first language.
>
> But after spending six weeks at Harvard, I don't think people should be in a program learning Navajo up till their senior year. Learning the English language is more valuable if you want to survive in the real world. I mean, most of the colleges are off-reservation, and if somebody wants to survive there, you have to know English really well—if you are going to communicate.
>
> Knowing Navajo is good, but where reading and writing are concerned, I don't think schools here should teach Navajo literacy. You waste a lot of time doing that, when you could be learning English. If any bilingual instruction is offered, it should only go up to the eighth grade; after that, there should only be English courses.*

She felt at the Rock Point High School she had not been taught to analyze teaching to firsthand experiences? Do I make use of the every-day things children do at school, and do I provide children with a wealth of experiences to enrich their background?"[18]

ESL teaching methods helped bring up students scores, but they remained two grade levels below the U.S. national averages, so Rock Point started a Navajo/English bilingual education

---

what she wrote; she just wrote from the "top of her head." She was dismayed to learn that she would have to take remedial writing and math courses as a freshman at Harvard.

Just as Maria had a difficult time moving from high school to a college or university, many students, especially minority students, deal with similar problems. In his book, *Lives on the Boundary*, Mike Rose describes how students can get "As" on their high school papers for summarizing assigned topics, but when they get to college the same paper can get a "D" or an "F" because the professors want more than a summary. Maria was told in her special summer program between her junior and senior year, "Think what you're writing. What are you saying? What is your thesis? Thesis, thesis, thesis: everything has to relate to your main topic." However, many students are not told this as clearly as Maria was, and they don't understand why the same type of writing they did for high school is no longer good enough. They often drop out of college when they can't come to terms with these new expectations.

Maria did not drop out. After her freshman year at Harvard, when she read a student's article criticizing Navajo language instruction in the Rock Point school newspaper, she wrote a long letter supporting Rock Point's bilingual program, telling students, "We need to learn how to deal with this assimilation process yet maintain our identity as Navajos. Be appreciative that [Rock Point] is trying to provide a medium so transitions from red to white and white to red will be easier."**

* Daniel McLaughlin, *When Literacy Empowers: Navajo Language in Print* (Albuquerque, N.M.: University of New Mexico Press, 1992), 8, 166.

** Ibid.

program in 1967, which remained limited until 1971, when the school received funds under the Bilingual Education Act passed by Congress in 1968 and signed by President Lyndon Johnson. Using *bilingual education*, students were taught subjects such as reading, mathematics, and science in their Native language, while also being taught to speak, read, and write English. To become qualified for Rock Point's bilingual education program, the school's teacher aides took college courses in the evenings and summers. These bilingual Navajo teachers had to adapt and write their own Navajo language materials. By the end of the 1980s, Rock Point only had one non-Navajo elementary teacher to that point, which is in sharp contrast to most reservation schools that continued to use mostly non-Native American teachers.

In 1972, a local school board was elected at Rock Point to provide "quality Navajo education through local community control," and in 1973 it contracted with the BIA to operate the school. Originally an elementary school, one grade a year was added from 1976 through 1982, when the first high school seniors graduated.

Under the new bilingual program, Rock Point kindergarten students were immersed in Navajo two-thirds of the time, while the other third was devoted to instruction in English. In grades one through four students had one-half day of Navajo instruction, which included instruction in math and science, and one-half day in English. From fifth grade to high school graduation, students spent about one-fifth of their class time in Navajo and the remainder in English. This type of program is called a maintenance or developmental bilingual program, because it maintains the students' Native language while they learn a second language. Instruction in math and science was hands-on, so that students could learn about these subjects while they were adjusting to English.

Rock Point's new bilingual program had excellent results. Even though students' English language test scores were lower in the early grades, when a lot of their lessons were taught in Navajo, in the upper grades, their test scores were higher because bilingual education allowed them to better understand what they were learning. By 1983, Rock Point's eighth graders were getting higher test scores on the California Achievement Test than other Native Americans in Arizona. In 1987, Rock Point students scored equal or better on the California Basic Education Skills Test than students at surrounding BIA schools. At the same time, Rock Point students were learning to read and write Navajo. In addition to high test scores, the success of Rock Point's bilingual program was further proved by student attendance rates that were above 94 percent. In contrast, Rough Rock's attendance rate was only around 75 percent. In addition, parent conference attendance rates at Rock Point rose to more than 80 percent and parents became more involved with the school through quarterly parent-teacher conferences, public meetings, an elected parent advisory committee that formally observed the school, school sponsored cultural events, and community dinners.

In 1988, 43 percent of students who entered Rock Point spoke mainly Navajo, while only 5 percent spoke English. This situation called for bilingual education, and University of New Mexico professor Bernard Spolsky declared in 1980 that "In a community that respects its own language but wishes its children to learn another, a good bilingual program that starts with the bulk of instruction in the child's native language and moves systematically toward" English, the students will do better than those taught only in English.[19]

Although assimilationists felt that speaking Native languages was unnecessary and that they were better forgotten, tribal members often had a different opinion. Navajo Tribal Chairman Peterson Zah declared in 1983, "No-one can fully participate in the affairs of the Navajo people without speaking Navajo" and he emphasized the importance of teaching Navajo in schools. Although bilingual education allowed some Navajo students to do better in school, they still had a lot of trouble doing well in college. The importance of building on the knowledge that students brought from home to school, including their tribal language was not new. A 1928 investigation of Indian education recommended that school curriculum be less assimilationist and based more on "local Indian life, or at least written within the scope of the child's early experiences."[20] Describing the impact of white culture and assimilationist education on Navajo, Harvard anthropologist Clyde Kluckhohn wrote in 1962, "Navajo culture is becoming an ugly patchwork of meaningless and unrelated pieces, whereas it was once a finely patterned mosaic."[21]

Because most Native Americans were pushed or forcefully removed from the eastern part of the United States, most Native Americans today live in the West, but some Native Americans remain in the East and like their western brothers are trying to revive the languages of their ancestors, some of which are no longer spoken and must be learned from early records and from other groups who speak similar dialects. Mohawks in northern New York State and southern Ontario have developed an immersion program in their Akwesasne Freedom School, which was started in 1980 by parents and individuals worried about the lack of traditional/cultural teaching in the mainstream schools and the inaccurate Mohawk and Native American history taught in them. Parents created a school run by consensus in which every decision that affected the school would result from parental discussion. Their Website declares, "We wanted our children to be proud of who they are, to know their culture and history and to speak our native language."[22] In the West, where most tribes outside of California have more speakers, revitalization efforts for some tribes have extended into the college level, as has taken place in New Zealand and Hawaii, which is described in chapter 4.

NAVAJO COMMUNITY COLLEGE

The failure of mainstream colleges and universities to recruit and retain Native American students led to the exploration of alternative routes to higher education for Native Americans. In 1957, the Navajo tribe established a scholarship fund financed by oil wells on the reservation. However, more than 50 percent of the students dropped out in their freshman year. This high dropout rate prompted Navajo leaders to explore the possibility of setting up their own college. In the early 1960s, Navajo educator Dillon Platero; traditional elder and chairman of the Tribal Council's Education Committee, Allen Yazzie; and tribal council delegate, Guy Gorman worked to establish a Navajo college as a solution to the problem of these high dropout rates in non-Indian colleges. In 1965, they convinced the OEO to initiate a study that concluded that a tribally controlled community college should be established.

With the example of RRDS in mind, meetings were held and Robert Roessel was brought into the planning process. A proposal was submitted to the OEO at the start of 1968, and with Navajo Tribal Chairman Raymond Nakai's strong support, the Navajo Tribal Council passed a resolution founding Navajo Community College (NCC). Roessel stepped down from directing RRDS and became NCC's first president. Three hundred and nine students enrolled in January 1969 in the BIA high school building at Many Farms, Arizona, and approximately 60 percent passed that first semester, which was a large improvement from previous percentages of Native American students attending non-Native American colleges. By 1978, NCC's enrollment had reached 1,241 students.

An advocate of local control, Roessel soon stepped aside as president of NCC, and in July 1969, Dr. Ned Hatathli became NCC's first Navajo president. Both Roessel and Hatathli envisioned Navajo studies as the centerpiece of the college and intended to replace non-Native American staff, as qualified Native Americans became available. In 1971, the U.S. Congress

Peter MacDonald, who served as Navajo tribal chairman from 1971 to 1983 and again from 1987 to 1989, was a supporter of raising the admission standards at Navajo Community College and making it more like non-Indian colleges. NCC, now known as Diné College, was the first college established for Native Americans by Native Americans, when it was founded in 1968.

passed the Navajo Community College Act to provide federal support for the college. Yazzie Begay donated family lands at Tsaile, Arizona, and ground was broken in 1971 for the construction of a permanent campus, which opened in 1973; branch campuses were soon established in Navajo population centers, including Shiprock, Tuba City, and Chinle.

On the one hand, Native American activists reject much of mainstream thinking on what should be included in college curriculum. They want to emphasize tribal languages, history, and culture. Other Native Americans want tribal colleges to offer the same curriculum as non-Native American colleges so that students can transfer to them easily or could graduate from a tribal college and get a good job. This conflict over the role of tribal colleges soon surfaced at NCC. Tribal traditionalists saw NCC playing a leading role in preserving tribal culture, although modernists saw NCC as a place to prepare students to get jobs or to leave the reservation for more education.

After Hatathli's death in 1972, the new president, Thomas Atcitty, moved NCC, with the support of the new tribal chairman, Peter MacDonald, toward a more traditional non-Native American community college. In his autobiography, MacDonald describes growing up herding sheep and

Navajo Code Talkers

Navajo "Code Talkers" served in the Pacific Theater during World War II and used a radio code based on their Navajo language that the Japanese were unable to break, unlike other codes the U.S. Marines used. The Navajo language-based code allowed Marine units to communicate with each other over their radios without the Japanese knowing what was said, which saved the lives of many U.S. soldiers. Code Talkers were in constant danger and not just from their enemies. They could be mistaken for Japanese infiltrators and shot by their fellow Marines because of their skin color and facial features.

Originally kept as a military secret, the Code Talkers went unrecognized for their contribution to the U.S. war effort for many years. It was not until July 2001 that the original twenty-nine Code Talkers received Congressional Gold Medals of Honor for their valuable service; only five were still alive. The other four hundred Navajo Code Talkers received Congressional Silver Medals of Honor posthumously.

attending a BIA day school. Later, he ran away from boarding school twice because of the teasing, taunting, and regimentation and dropped out of school in sixth grade. MacDonald enlisted in the U.S. Marine Corps near the end of World War II and trained as a "Code Talker."

After the war, MacDonald was allowed to enroll at Bacone—at that time a Baptist Indian junior college in Oklahoma—on the GI bill, despite his lack of a high school education. The GI bill provided government scholarships to World War II veterans so they could receive a college education. After getting a General Equivalency Diploma (GED) at Bacone, MacDonald majored in sociology and studied both Christianity and Native American history. After graduating from Bacone, he majored in engineering at the University of Oklahoma. He worked nights at the state mental hospital and was encouraged by the BIA to enter a trade school when his veteran benefits ran out. MacDonald chose instead to work two years to save enough money so that he could return to the University of Oklahoma and complete his electrical engineering degree, which he did in 1957.

After being recruited by several companies, MacDonald went to work for Hughes Aircraft. His autobiography describes a successful career at Hughes, where he learned about missiles and other cutting-edge technology. He also learned to be a "jet-setter" and was impressed by the rich lifestyle of the corporate chief executive officers (CEOs) at Hughes. Despite opportunities for promotion at Hughes, Navajo Tribal chairman Raymond Nakai convinced MacDonald to head up OEO Programs on the Navajo Reservation. MacDonald used his OEO position to gain political support, and he defeated Nakai in the 1971 tribal election, replacing him as tribal chairman. As chairman, he worked to free the tribal government from BIA control and to negotiate better deals for the sale of the tribe's oil, gas, and coal deposits. He wrote in his autobiography:

Looking back, I realize that the BIA program was poorly planned and unrelated to the needs of the Navajo children. The hostile attitude toward my people was emotionally devastating, of course. We were taught that we were superstitious savages, and we were forced to go to church without being given an understanding of the Christian religion. We were made to feel that our parents, our grandparents, and everyone who had come before us was inferior. . . . We were constantly told that we were truly inferior to them and that we would always be inferior.[23]

Despite his words, it was obvious from his actions that MacDonald appreciated the finer things in life and wanted the Navajo elite to have the same luxuries as non-Native Americans. He and his wife sponsored a Navajo academy for the best high school students, but he went to jail in 1990 for accepting bribes and helping incite a riot after the tribal council attempted to remove him from office. At the request of a new Navajo tribal council, U.S. President William J. Clinton pardoned MacDonald; releasing him from jail just before he left office in 2001.

MacDonald wanted NCC to be more like non-Indian colleges, and admission standards were instituted to improve the quality of matriculating students. Roessel and his supporters resented the fact that under MacDonald's administration, Navajo studies were no longer a separate program at NCC. NCC's sixth president, Dean C. Jackson, who served from 1979 to 1989, promoted a "Diné Philosophy of Learning," which is described by the college:

The educational philosophy of Diné College is Sa'ah Naagháí Bik'eh Hózhóón, the Diné traditional living system, which places human life in harmony with the natural world and the universe. The philosophy provides principles both for protection from the imperfections in life and for the development of well being.[24]

At times, in reaction to the many years of coercive assimilation in BIA schools that devalued all that was Native American, tribally controlled schools could turn to the other extreme and devalue everything that was "white." Deborah House, who took both Navajo studies classes and taught at NCC in the 1990s, wrote in her book, *Language Shift among the Navajos*, that at NCC, non-Native American students were encouraged to criticize their own upbringing and cultures. Their "language, literature, religion, family life, and ethnic identities" were regularly devalued by Navajo and non-Navajo instructors, administrators, and other students. House found that although there was a lot of talk about the importance of revitalizing Navajo language and culture at NCC, far less was actually being done to address the issue. The ideal Navajo lifestyle that was promoted in some NCC classes of "sheepherding and growing a small garden, living in a Hogan [a traditional hexagonal one room Navajo home], and driving a team of horses" was not realistic for most Navajos due to the immense increase in Navajo population over the previous century. The new Navajo horse and wagon is the pickup truck, which requires a job to earn money to pay for gas and car payments.[25]

In 1996, a four-year teacher education program was started at NCC, in cooperation with Arizona State University. The program emphasizes preparing teachers to teach bilingually, and graduates are required to read and write Navajo, as well as English. In 1997, NCC was renamed Diné College. Diné means "the people" in the Navajo language and is their name for themselves. The school's enrollment averaged 1,387 students per semester between 1997 and 2002—much higher than any of the other tribal colleges.

OTHER TRIBAL COLLEGES

Other tribes soon chartered tribal colleges that followed the Navajos' example. D-Q (Deganawidah-Quetzalcoatl)

University near Davis, California, was formed in 1971 as a joint Hispanic-Indian school. Jack D. Forbes (Powhatan and Delaware) helped found the California Indian Education Association in 1967, which worked to create an Indian college for California Native American students. After a nonviolent takeover of an abandoned army installation near Davis, California, the founders were able to get the facility turned over to the college. But funding in the early years was uncertain. The students were mainly urban Native Americans, and Lakota was the only Native American language taught at the college. The activist nature of the founders was reflected by the presence of American Indian Movement (AIM) leader Dennis Banks as an instructor in 1975 and an assistant to the president in 1976. (Banks' employment was a condition set by then California Governor Jerry Brown to keep him from being sent to South Dakota to face criminal charges stemming from the second Wounded Knee takeover.) In 1978, the Hispanic board members were forced to resign so that the college could get funding through the Tribal College Act.

Oglala Lakota College (OLC) on the Pine Ridge Reservation in South Dakota was founded in 1969 by volunteers in association with the University of Colorado. Its 1978 mission statement proclaimed that its trustees stressed "the importance of maintaining the Lakota culture and fostering tribal self determination," although also preparing students "to understand the ways of the larger society." In order to better serve the dispersed communities on the reservation, the college had nine centers rather than one central campus. The college's 2001 vision statement for its four-year teacher preparation program stated:

> To graduate highly qualified, professional, motivated, committed teachers who possess and who will teach Wolakota in a multicultural, changing world [Wolakota refers to the whole person in balance and in harmony spiritually, physically, mentally and socially].[26]

OLC's goal for students is that they:

1) Have the ability to develop and maintain an individual wellness program, nurture the mind, body, heart and spirit.
2) Have the ability to model self-identity, founded on cultural practices, customs, values and beliefs.
3) Be able to demonstrate basic understanding and usage of the Lakota language.
4) Be able to demonstrate community involvement or service.
5) Reflect and document real life examples of character (courage, honesty, generosity, etc.).
6) Demonstrate and document effective communication skills.
7) Demonstrate and document professional abilities of critical thinking and problem solving.[27]

Sinte Gleska College on the Rosebud Sioux Reservation in South Dakota was chartered in 1971 and began with six centers. From the beginning, Sinte Gleska had a large non-Native American enrollment, sometimes representing more than 50 percent of the student body. One of the founders of the college, Gerald Mohatt, went on to help form the American Indian Higher Education Consortium (AIHEC) in 1972. AIHEC supports the publication of *Tribal College*, a quarterly journal that publishes news about tribal colleges and has an annual student edition. In 1972, Lionel Bordeaux (Rosebud Sioux) became Sinte Gleska's president, a position he still holds in 2005.

AMERICAN INDIAN AND NATIVE AMERICAN STUDIES

In the 1950s, the BIA enticed many Native Americans to relocate to cities with the promise of employment. Unfortunately, the BIA's promises were often unfounded and some disappointed relocatees became community activists, as happened in

San Francisco with the Alcatraz Island takeover from 1969 to 1971. Alcatraz Island, also known as "the Rock," was originally set up as an army prison, and nineteen Hopi Indians who refused to send their children to school were imprisoned there in 1895. From 1934 to 1963 it was a maximum security federal prison where notorious criminals like Al Capone and Machine Gun Kelly were sent. When it was closed, some Native American activists demanded that it be returned to the Native Americans who originally owned it before the military took it over. Many of the activists who took over Alcatraz were college students from the University of California–Berkeley, the University of California–Los Angeles, and San Francisco State College.

Though the South Dakota State Legislature authorized the founding of an Institute of American Indian Studies at the University of South Dakota in 1955, in response to calls by university administrators and Native American representatives, Native American Studies (NAS) programs did not become part of the university curriculum until the 1970s. These programs, largely founded at the California universities mentioned above, offered courses in Native American literature, American Indian legal-political studies, Native American arts, Native American religion and philosophy, Native American education, American Indian languages, American Indian tribal and community development, and related areas. Jack D. Forbes, who helped found the University of California–Davis' NAS program, wrote that the "thrust of Indian Studies is not primarily to study the Indian community but to develop practical programs for and by the Indian community."[28] Academics, like Forbes, also supported the growth of tribal colleges.

GROWTH OF TRIBAL SCHOOLS AND COLLEGES

The growth of the number of tribal schools and colleges in the last three decades indicates the vitality of Native American people today. In 2004, about half the 185 elementary and secondary schools funded by the BIA were tribally controlled and there were thirty-four tribal colleges and universities in the United States, plus several in Canada. However, these tribal schools and colleges remain poorly funded, often in crumbling or temporary buildings. Both tribal schools and colleges continue to perform a balancing act between looking like regular non-Native American institutions and supporting Native heritages. American Indian studies programs are caught in a balancing act between "ivory tower" academic study (with no immediate use) and providing a practical education that students can immediately use. Longtime Sinte Gleska College president Lionel Bordeaux expressed the view that the founders of tribal colleges "foresaw the need to preserve the Indian culture so cultural preservation is really the foundation of the tribal colleges."

In the 1990s, there was a move by some tribal colleges to become four-year institutions. Sinte Gleska College became a university in 1992, and it and Oglala Lakota College in South Dakota developed four-year teacher preparation programs. Sinte Gleska also developed a master's program in education. Both Diné College in Arizona and Haskell Indian Nations University in Lawrence, Kansas, began developing teacher education programs in the mid-1990s. Haskell started off as a boarding school in 1884, teaching teenagers to be farmers and only providing an elementary education. Its growth into a university today reflects the great strides made in Native American education over the last century.

3

Native American Identity

S uccess in school and in life is related to people's identity; how they are viewed as a group and individually by others and how they see themselves. Identity is not just a positive self-concept. It is finding your place in the world with both humility and strength. It is, in the words of Vine Deloria (Standing Rock Sioux), "accepting the responsibility to be a contributing member of a society." It is children as they grow up finding a "home in the landscapes and ecologies they inhabit."[29] In their 2003 study of Native American youth titled *The Seventh Generation*, Amy Bergstrom, Linda Cleary, and Thomas Peacock found that "Identity development from an Indigenous perspective has less to do with striving for individualism and more to do with establishing connections and understanding ourselves in relation to all the things around us."[30]

Children also need to develop the *inner direction* described by sociologist David Riesman to build a strong identity that helps them

The next day the torture began. The first thing they did was cut our hair....While we were bathing our breechclouts were taken, and we were ordered to put on trousers. We'd lost our hair and we'd lost our clothes; with the two we'd lost our identity as Indians.

Margaret Archuleta, the curator of fine art for the Heard Museum, stands next to a barber chair that is part of the Phoenix museum's exhibit "Remembering Our Indian School Days: The Boarding School Experience." For Native Americans, long hair was often an important symbol of personal identity and the barber chair represents a time when many Native Americans were sent to Indian schools to be assimilated into Euro-American society.

withstand the onslaughts of a negative pleasure-seeking and materialistic popular TV and Hollywood movie culture, fears engendered by terrorism, the temptations of alcohol and drugs, and the pervasive culture of poverty that envelopes many reservations and inner cities. Teachers need to help children develop resilience so they can bounce back from the negative experiences that they, and all of us, are sure to face in life.

The common transmission, or *direct instruction*, teaching approach using lectures and textbooks that forms the indoctrinating teaching methods and materials of many schools today does not help develop truly strong identities. Rather, giving students an engaging educational framework where they can thoughtfully experience and interact with their social and physical environment produces in them a strong personal and cultural identity. University of Toronto professor Jim Cummins describes this as transformative teaching, which enables "students to relate curriculum content to their individual and collective experience and to analyze broader social issues relevant to their lives."[31] This is a joint learning experience that involves both students and teachers in the learning process.

Cummins believes that teachers must learn from their students, as well as having the students learn from them. In their 1998 book on Native American education titled *Collected Wisdom: American Indian Education*, Linda Cleary and Thomas Peacock emphasized this theme of "teacher as learner." Teachers need to learn about the lives of their students beyond the school grounds so that they may also learn more about the home language and culture of their students and better understand the challenges their students face in their lives.

Educators not only need to teach academics but also help students retain and develop their identity as members of an ethnic group, as Americans, and as citizens of the world. Instructional methodology and curriculum are not the only variables that lead to academic success for students. A key factor for academic success is how students, parents, and communities view themselves and schools. Ideally, they need to change the meaning and content of the curriculum so that students can see it as true education and part of their maturational process as human beings, rather than feeling that they are being indoctrinated and assimilated.

In this process, it is important to determine whether or not teachers are viewed as enemies or friends. Are teachers enemies who are seeking to erase their students' Native American cultures or friends seeking to build students' tribal identities; acquainting them to the wider world in which they will spend their lives? National standards, high-stakes testing, and the passage of antibilingual education "English for the Children" propositions in California in 1998, in Arizona in 2000, and Massachusetts in 2002 all push teachers to ignore Indian students' uniqueness and provide a one-size-fits-all assimilationist curriculum that ignores the psychological needs of children as they are growing up.

OTHER BARRIERS TO SUCCESS

The actual situation in some minority communities can be like the one Larry Colton describes in *Counting Coup*, when a Crow high school basketball star, her grandmother, and the rest of her extended family (her aunts, uncles, cousins, etc.) failed to realize that basketball, football, rodeo, and owning a car are not substitutes for education, whether traditional or modern. On the other hand, academics alone do not provide a full education. Grandma will probably not enthusiastically support schooling if she perceives that her grandchild will move hundreds, if not thousands, of miles away to get a job once educated; leaving her with no one to chop her firewood and take her to town for groceries. She may also want to see and be near her great-grandchildren. The definition of being Native American (or a member of some other ethnic group) and educated must extend beyond sports and other limited definitions, and should be strengthened with traditional wisdom that should be the foundation of America's educational system.

Ethnic groups justifiably tend to focus on their traditional moral and spiritual strengths; however, it is important, as Haskell professor Daniel Wildcat (Muskogee/Creek) notes, not to "romanticize the past." There is a danger that Native Americans and other minority groups can, in fact, as House found at Diné College, define themselves as the "white man's shadow"; the mirror opposite of the perceived selfish, material-istic, and individualistic Euro-American man. Instead of plac-ing the blame on themselves for their problems, Native Americans may "blame the oppressor" for everything that is going wrong in their life and community.

Although there is no question that Native Americans have suffered a lot at the hands of European immigrants and their descendants, there is a danger for students who believe in this "oppositional identity." Subjects such as reading, writing, and mathematics, which are increasingly critical for economic sur-vival, can be seen as un-Indian, "acting white," and "selling out" to the white man. Although past history should not be forgot-ten, neither should the many instances of whites trying to help Native Americans and vice versa. As Metis historian David T. McNab recalled hearing at the Toronto International Pow-Wow in 2000, "The Elders tell us that it is all right to feel angry about stuff like this [the Sand Creek Massacre] and it is good. However, in the end you must go down to the river, offer a gift of tobacco to the Creator and simply let the anger go. . . . Otherwise the anger will poison your spirit. . . ." Living with anger either bottled up or unexpressed is unhealthy, and a process of healing needs to take place. This does not mean that as part of the educational process students should forget their past and not learn how to fight for their rights. The late University of California professor John U. Ogbu recommended that educators realize that Native American and other *involun-tary minority* children (not children of immigrant parents who have come to the United States as the "land of opportunity") can have *oppositional identities* in regard to schooling. In order to achieve success, one must make a decision to learn, despite all the cultural insensitivity that can be displayed in schools, but one need not assimilate.

In a 1995 paper titled "Understanding Cultural Diversity and Learning," Ogbu recommended that teachers study the his-tory and cultural adaptations of their students' ethnic groups, have special counseling programs to help students separate attitudes and behaviors enhancing school success from those that lead to linear acculturation or "acting white," and promote "accommodation without assimilation" or "playing the classroom game." He further recommended that minority communities, which of course include Native American tribes, should:

1) Teach children to separate attitudes and behaviors that lead to academic success from those that lead to a loss of ethnic identity, culture, and language;
2) Show children clearly that the family, community [and tribe] value academic success in schools;
3) Insist "children recognize and accept the responsibility for their school adjustment and academic performance"; and
4) Educational success should not be seen as a "ticket out" to leave one's community behind.[32]

DROPOUTS

Recent research on Native American dropouts illustrates how students give up on school because they perceive their teachers to be uncaring and do not see the relevance in what they are being taught. In a 1992 *Journal of American Indian Education* article, University of Utah professor Donna Deyhle quotes a Native American student:

> The way I see it seems like the whites don't want to get involved with the Indians. They think we're bad. We drink. Our families drink. Dirty. Ugly. And the teachers don't want to help us. They say, "Oh, no, there is another Indian asking a question" because they don't understand. So we stop asking questions.[33]

She quotes another student:

> It was just like they [teachers] want to put us aside, us Indians. They didn't tell us nothing about careers or things

to do after high school. They didn't encourage us to go to college. They just took care of the white students. They just wanted to get rid of the Indians.[34]

Deyhle found that Navajo high school graduates in southeastern Utah did not make more money than dropouts; though more of the graduates had jobs. She also documented the pervasive discrimination that Navajos faced both in and outside of school.

Research conducted for the Indian Nations at Risk Task Force found that the common assumption as to why Native students dropped out (because they are failing academically or having trouble with drugs and alcohol) was not accurate. Studies done with Navajo students by Deyhle and Navajo researcher Paul Platero found that the most frequent reason given by students for dropping out of school was that it was boring. They got tired of being told to read the textbook, often written a couple of grade levels above their reading ability, and being told to answer the questions at the end of the chapter. Students saw teachers, who seemed more interested in the subject matter they taught than in their students, as uncaring.

The 1986 Navajo Tribe's Dropout Study found that "the most successful students were for the most part fluent Navajo/English bilinguals and most dropouts were thinking about returning to school." A 1990 study by Montana State University professor Ruey-Lin Lin, which was published in the *Journal of American Indian Education*, found that Native American college students with traditional orientations outperform students with modern orientations. Traditionally oriented students were able to learn in school; overcoming the negative characteristics of the schools because of the strong sense of personal and group identity their Native culture gave them. Lin Lin also found in his studies that Native American students were more likely than white students to get ahead in the world by luck than by hard work. However, as the saying goes, many find that "the harder they work the luckier they get."

More than a decade ago, I reviewed research on dropouts for the U.S. Secretary of Education's Indian Nations at Risk Task Force.[35] In that review I focused mostly on "school-based" reasons for students dropping out of school. My review indicated that the large impersonal schools, the perception that teachers did not care, passive teaching methods, culturally irrelevant curriculum, inappropriate testing, tracked classes, and schools not involving parents contributed to the relatively high dropout rate for Native American and other minority students. I chose to focus on school-based reasons, because I did not want to use the "blame the victim" as an excuse, and I thought that these issues were the ones that policy makers and school officials could have some control over; in contrast to home-based reasons that were beyond the reach of schools.

However, it turns out I was too optimistic about schools making changes to improve the chances of academic success for Native American and other minority students. This has been demonstrated in the ongoing attacks on bilingual education and the increasing use of high-stakes testing to determine if students should be promoted to the next grade or allowed to graduate. *High-stakes tests* are one-size-fits-all exams, which states adopt and require all students to take. They are "high stakes" because students who do not score high enough are flunked or denied high school diplomas.

It goes without saying that students who are learning English can have a difficult time with English language tests, but there are other problems as well. Three stories from the Navajo Reservation provide examples of how students can get a test question "wrong" and be right. When my wife was teaching Navajo kindergarten students in Chinle, they took a test that required them to match an animal to a pond of water. Two of the animals were a cow and a duck. Most of the Navajo students matched the cow with the pond rather than picking the "right" answer—the duck. This was because they usually see cows gathered around the local ponds to drink rather than ducks swimming on them. In Kayenta, another Navajo community, students matched an umbrella to the sun rather than with rain; again missing the correct answer. It does not rain much in Kayenta but the sun shines a lot and when grandmother is out herding sheep, she uses her umbrella to keep from getting sunburned. The third example is from Cameron, which is a small town between Flagstaff and Page, Arizona. Navajo students were asked to match a boat with several choices, including a lake and a highway. Some students matched boats with the highway because when they looked out their classroom window they could see boats being towed up the highway to Lake Powell on the Colorado River. In the January 2004 issue of the journal *Phi Delta Kappan*, Rita Platt, who taught in Alaska, gives similar examples. One question on a test asked, "Which of these would most likely take you to the hospital if you got hurt?" and lists as possible answers:

1) An ambulance
2) A boat
3) A bicycle
4) An airplane

The "right" answer is of course an ambulance, but in Alaska there aren't any highways near Native villages, and if you are injured, you are taken to the hospital in an airplane. Native students in the Alaskan Arctic face many challenges in understanding things in their textbooks; having never seen firsthand a lawn mower, a forest, or many of the other things we assume children have seen and experienced.

Given the push to require all students to use the same textbooks and take the same tests, I believe that those of us who want minorities to achieve greater academic success are going to have to follow the lead of Ogbu and focus more on what minority students, their parents, and their communities can do to promote academic success and overcome the negative aspects of many schools.

For three decades Ogbu studied why some minorities do well in U.S. schools and others do not. His last study, *Black American Students in an Affluent Suburb*, focused on trying to understand why middle-class black students who lived in a prosperous suburban school district were not as academically successful as middle-class white students. Through interviews and classroom observations, he observed how students behaved in and out of class. He found that some minority groups are more successful academically in U.S. schools than others. He differentiated between voluntary (immigrant) minorities, including many Asian immigrants, who do well and involuntary minorities, including blacks and Native Americans, who do not do as well. Voluntary minorities see the United States as the "land of opportunity" and schooling as a path to economic advancement; while doing well in school was equated by some black students with "acting white," and "once individuals exceeded the level expected of them, other blacks in the community would begin to criticize them." This is similar to the "Bucket of Crabs" story that I have heard a number of times at Indian education conferences. When one crab tries to escape the bucket (the poverty on many Indian reservations), the other crabs pull it back in. Students with oppositional identities to white culture and schools tended to suffer academically, while students with home cultures that were viewed as just different from the culture of the school could do quite well.

Although Ogbu found some school-based reasons for black students performing at a below-average level—such as counselors having too many students to deal with to provide much individual attention—many of the challenges he found were in the students themselves and their families. Some black students did not know why they needed to learn math, and they did not believe that their present schooling prepared them for future jobs. Some students thought that they would become as well off financially as their educated middle-class parents; no matter how well they did in school.

Some teachers had low expectations for black students, but the students' role in forming these expectations, high or low, needs to be considered. Ogbu found that the actions of some black students accounted for some of their teachers' low expectations. Black students did not raise their hands as much as white students and were more likely to come to class without having done their homework. Black students were more likely to be distracted from classroom academics than white students, and Ogbu found a "norm of minimal effort" among some middle and high school blacks. "It was not cool to work hard in school." Other things were more important, including shopping at the mall and sports. Shopping, or consumerism, led students from middle-class families to take part-time jobs so they could have cell phones, computer games, and stylish clothes; although sports could also distract students from their school work. Ogbu's research confirmed other studies that found that "some black students invested so much time in sports that they had little time for their academic schoolwork" and "for some students, playing sports was all that mattered." The media promotes students' consumerism and obsession with sports, making "athletes, entertainers, drug dealers and their success, wealth, or reputations more visible than black doctors, lawyers, and other professionals."

Ogbu found that some black parents did not recognize the importance of their role in their children's success at school. They limited themselves "to putting pressure on teachers to do their job of teaching well; that is, limited to pushing teachers and other school personnel to educate their children." Ogbu found "dismal" black parent involvement, both at school and at home. Although there is a history of "collective mistreatment" shared by involuntary minorities, including Native Americans, Hispanics, and blacks that influences their view of white people and white institutions, including schools, the mistrust engendered by this history can hurt students' chances for doing well in school. The emphasis on discrimination, "on breaking the barriers in education and in the opportunity structure," led to ignoring "the behavior and attitudes that are conducive to school success."[36]

Ogbu did not recommend minority students assimilate in order to be academically successful. He found that minorities can accommodate to "white" schools without assimilating and that students could successfully learn and use standard English, which is needed to achieve success in the classroom, while also continuing to speak their home and community language, whether it is a tribal language, Indian English, Spanish, or Ebonics.

The late Alan Peshkin's 1997 study of a tribally controlled boarding school in New Mexico, titled *Places of Memory: Whitman's Schools and Native American Communities*, also tackles the question of why Native American students' academic achievement is below average, even in Native American-controlled schools. According to Peshkin, Native Americans have the lowest ACT college entrance scores and the highest dropout rate of any New Mexico ethnic group. He found that 75 percent of Native American students who go to college leave in their first year.

At the high school Peshkin studied, low academic performance was not the result of a lack of funding; the school received a combination of Bureau of Indian Affairs (BIA) funding and various federal grants, was staffed with well-educated teachers, and had adequate facilities and textbooks. The school also had the highest percentage of Native American teachers of any high school in New Mexico. In addition, Peshkin found that the students' parents valued education.

Peshkin spent a year as an observer at this New Mexico boarding school, which served the state's Pueblo Indians. The school met State of New Mexico accreditation standards, and its goal was to prepare students for college. But success was limited. Students would participate with sustained effort and enthusiasm in basketball, but "regrettably, I saw no academic counterpart to this stellar athletic performance." Peshkin wrote:

> In class, students generally were well-behaved and respectful. They were not rude, loud, or disruptive. More often they were indifferent . . . teachers could not get students to work hard consistently, to turn in assignments, to participate in class, or to take seriously . . . their classroom performance.[37]

Peshkin espoused the *cultural discontinuity* (two worlds) theory of academic failure to explain why these students did not enthusiastically embrace education. Cultural discontinuity refers to a mismatch of expectations between the students' home culture and the culture of the school, which leads to misunderstandings and student failure. In addition, Pueblo Indians distrust schools. Based on more than four hundred years of contact with European immigrants, the Pueblos have good reason to be suspicious of anything "white," and schools, even Native American-controlled ones with Native American administrators and Native American teachers, are still basically alien/foreign institutions as far as Pueblo culture is concerned.

Pueblo Indians are under cultural attack from all the forces of the majority society and are obsessed with cultural survival. Pueblo culture emphasizes fitting into the group and participating in the life of the village—"standing in" versus "standing out"—in contrast to the individualism found outside the Pueblo. "Schooling is necessary to become competent in the very world that Pueblo people perceive as rejecting them"; school is a place of "becoming white."[38]

According to Peshkin, "imbued with the ideal of harmony in their community life, Pueblo parents send their children to schools that promote cultural jangle."[39] The sounds in the school are not discordant. The discordance is between what the Pueblo communities teach their young and what the schools teach, and this discordance goes far beyond just the matter of teaching Pueblo languages in the home and English in schools.

Daniel McLaughlin's 1992 study of the Rock Point community and its bilingual school—*When Literacy Empowers*—presented a very different picture than Peshkin's study. The bilingual curriculum at Rock Point "Indianized" its curriculum much more completely than in the school Peshkin studied. In contrast to Navajos, Pueblos have resisted learning to write their languages, which has probably been strengthened because the initial supporters of Native language writing were missionaries who used reading and writing as a quick way to introduce Native Americans to the Bible, catechisms, hymns, and other materials in their own language in order to promote conversion to Christianity. However, attitudes are changing. The Hopis of Arizona initially opposed writing their language and having it taught in schools, but now that fewer of their children are speaking Hopi, they are asking that it be taught.

It is troubling to observe schooling being perceived as a "white" or "Anglo" institution that, if whole heartily embraced, threatens Native American tribal and family values. Perhaps the answer lies in the examination of education in Asian and other non-white and non-European cultures, which offer a broader perspective than U.S. schools. The negative effects of viewing education as "white" is illustrated in a series of studies of American Indian college students that was conducted by Professor Terry Huffman and published in 2001 in Arizona State University's *Journal of American Indian Education.* He found that students' collective identity is critical to their academic success. Native American students who attend college often find little there with which to relate and consequently suffer feelings of alienation. Some of these students quickly became disillusioned and drop out; seeing schooling as a means to assimilate them to white culture. Others persist, drawing personal strength from their Native heritage and learning to relate to white culture, using their traditional culture as an anchor.

Although it is a mistake to believe that schools are devoid of problems, it is also a mistake to believe that they are the root of the problem and that minority students are victims who cannot individually fight and overcome the educational odds. University of Montana professor Dr. Steve Greymorning (Arapaho) has described the courage that students need to show; equating them with Cheyenne Indian Dog Soldiers, who pledged their lives as warriors to protect their people. When in battle they were often the first line of defense, standing between the advancing enemy and their people. Stories are told how they would tie a leather thong around their leg; the other end attached to an arrow or a wooden spike that was driven into the ground. From this position they defended the people, and by this act Cheyenne Dog Soldiers helped to ensure the continuation of both their tribe and culture.

Greymorning argues that students need to show some of this courage when battling discrimination and misunderstanding both in and out of schools. In *The Seventh Generation*, Bergstrom, Cleary, and Peacock found that only a few of the schools they visited were "comfortable places for Native students to learn."

Although courage can help Native American students overcome negative school experiences, their extended families can also help. Ogbu recommends that minority communities take advantage of and promote organizations that support students' academic success, such as the American Indian Science and Engineering Society (AISES), which publishes the *Winds of Change* magazine, and the Society for Advancement of Chicanos and Native Americans (SACNAS), which has an online biography project that describes the accomplishments of Chicano/Latino and Native American scientists. These organizations can help connect students who are interested in becoming scientists with mentors.

Although one should be careful about comparing black and other minority students to Native American students, one should also understand that the experiences of Native American students are not unique and that they face some of the same challenges that other American minorities and indigenous children face throughout the world.

DR. LORI ARVISO ALVORD[40]

Lori Arviso Alvord is an example of a Native American who has achieved success and can be emulated by Native American students. Alvord's Navajo father met her white mother while he was in the armed forces, and she was born in a military hospital in Tacoma, Washington. Neither of her parents completed college. In her 1999 autobiography, *The Scalpel and the Silver Bear*, she describes her journey from the Crownpoint public schools on the Navajo Reservation, to Dartmouth College, then to Stanford University Medical School, and finally to being the first Navajo woman surgeon. It was not an easy trip. She writes:

> I made good grades in high school, but I had received a very marginal education. I had a few good teachers, but teachers were difficult to recruit to our schools and they often did not stay long. Funding was inadequate. I spent many hours in classrooms where, I now see, very little was being taught.[41]

A friend encouraged her to apply to Dartmouth, an Ivy League college in New Hampshire that was established in 1769 to provide education and instruction to the youth of the Indian tribes of what would later become the United States. Unfortunately for Alvord, the education she received on the reservation left her "totally unprepared for the physical and life sciences. After receiving the only D of my entire life in calculus, I retreated from the sciences altogether."[42]

What saved her from dropping out was her "strong reading background." She writes, "I read my way through the tiny local library and the vans that came to our community from the

Dr. Lori Arviso Alvord, the first Navajo woman to be a board-certified surgeon, combines the use of Western medicine with traditional Navajo healing techniques. Dr. Alvord is shown here at a 1999 book signing in Santa Fe, New Mexico, shortly after the release of *The Scalpel and the Silver Bear*. In the book, Alvord describes her journey from the Crownpoint public schools on the Navajo Reservation, to Dartmouth College, then to Stanford University Medical School.

Books on Wheels program"; she was also encouraged by her parents "to read and dream."[43] During her childhood, she could even get out of chores by reading.

She majored in the social sciences and graduated from Dartmouth in 1979. Not being able to get a job in Crownpoint, she went to Albuquerque, where she was offered two jobs, one as a social worker and another paying much less as a medical research assistant at the University of New Mexico. She accepted the lower-paying job and became increasingly interested in medicine, enrolling at the University of New Mexico, where she was encouraged by her advisor to take the math and science classes she had avoided at Dartmouth. Alvord used her newfound success in math and science to gain acceptance to Stanford University's prestigious medical school.

Subject matter preparation was not the only problem she faced in college. "Navajos are taught from the youngest age never to draw attention to ourselves. So Navajo children do not raise their hands in class. At a school like Dartmouth, the lack of participation was not seen as a sign of humility but lack of interest and a disengaged attitude."[44] Later in medical school, she was perceived as being "remote and disinterested" for similar reasons.

In many Native American cultures, humility rather than individualism is emphasized. When teachers call on students to answer questions in class they are "spotlighting" those students and possibly embarrassing them. Native American students do not want to outshine their fellow students by appearing to know more than them. Japanese culture also espouses humility, and there is a Japanese saying that states: "the nail that sticks out gets pounded down." In other words, if a Japanese person tries to appear superior to other Japanese, he/she is subjected to social pressure to conform and be like everyone else and not to stand out. In his book *Teaching the Native American*, Hap Gilliland tells a story of a Northern Cheyenne girl who stopped reading books in her class. The teacher was keeping a record of how many books each student read by putting gold stars on a chart on the classroom wall. When the girl's line of stars got way ahead of her classmates, she stopped reading so they could catch up.

Although Native Americans such as Susan LaFleshe (Omaha) and Charles Eastman (Sioux) have served as medical doctors for more than a century, one should not underestimate Dr. Alvord's accomplishments. Only 4 percent of the practicing surgeons in the United States are women, and only a few of those women are Native Americans. Although she was accepted into medical school partly because she was Native American and benefited from affirmative action, this meant that she had to prove herself. Alvord held herself to a higher standard, lest "My being a surgeon would be attributed to quota filling, not the result of hard work and my own merit."[45]

During her hospital residency, she credited a Pueblo Indian doctor for his help in teaching her how to be a caring doctor. A large part of her autobiography emphasizes how she worked to combine modern medical practice with traditional Navajo healing beliefs of walking in beauty and "living in balance and harmony." She also describes the pain brought to her by her dad's descent into alcoholism and ultimate death in an alcohol-related car crash, and the gruesome medical statistics of Navajo and other Native American deaths from automobile accidents; an estimated 60 percent of which are alcohol-related. As a surgeon, she operated on some of these accident victims.

To a degree she blames schools, which she saw as an arm of European-American colonialism, for what happened to her father. She describes how,

> In their childhoods both my father and my grandmother had been punished for speaking Navajo in school. Navajos were told by white educators that, in order to be successful, they would have to forget their language and culture and adopt American ways. They were warned that if they taught their children to speak Navajo, the children would have a harder time learning in school, and would therefore be at a disadvantage.[46]

A racist attitude existed. Navajo children were told that their culture and lifeways were inferior, and they were made to feel they could never be as good as White people. This pressure to assimilate, along with the physical, social, psychological, and economic destruction of the tribes following the Indian wars of the 1800s . . . combined to bring the Navajo people to their knees. . . .

My father suffered terribly from these events and conditions. He had been a straight-A student and was sent away to one of the best prep schools in the state. He wanted to be like the rich white children who surround him there, but the differences were too apparent.[47]

Dr. Alvord concludes that "two or three generations of our tribe had been taught to feel shame about our culture, and parents had often not taught their children traditional Navajo beliefs—the very thing that would have shown them how to live, the very thing that could keep them strong."[48] Because of these outdated attitudes, she was forced to study Navajo language as an adult to better serve her patients at Gallup Indian Medical Center in New Mexico. After a number of years practicing surgery in Gallup, Dr. Alvord returned to Dartmouth to work in its medical school as an associate dean, where she helps new doctors learn about the spiritual as well as the physical side of healing, which she learned from her Navajo culture and traditional Navajo healers.

4

Language and Culture Revitalization

The pace of assimilation for Native Americans, which government schools had promoted for more than a century, became more rapid as Indian reservations became less isolated, roads were paved, and more and more Native Americans bought cars, pickup trucks, and television sets. As the children watched English language programs on television, fewer and fewer of them learned their Native language. This experience of language loss is not unique to the United States. Other indigenous people, many of whom still live where their ancestors have lived for thousands of years, suffered language loss when colonial powers subjected them to their forms of education and then radio and television entered their homes. If indigenous people had accepted assimilation, it might have been OK to relegate indigenous languages and culture to museums. However, race prejudice has not disappeared, and many indigenous students still do not do well in assimilationist-oriented schools. With the

The revitalization of Native languages is an important part of maintaining tribal identity and some states, such as Oregon, have passed bills to allow tribal elders to teach their language in schools without having a teaching license or college degree. Shown here is Mildred Quaempts, a language teacher for the Confederated Tribes of the Umatilla Indian Reservation in Pendleton, Oregon. Quaempts is singing in the Sahaptin dialect of the Umatilla language to a class of preschool children.

promise of assimilation unfulfilled, indigenous people world-wide are looking to their past to restore their communities and heal the wounds of colonialism.[49]

A SUCCESS STORY: TE KOHANGA REO

The Maoris of New Zealand are one such indigenous group in which fewer and fewer children were speaking their ancestral language but were still not doing well in schools. The Maoris make up about 15 percent of New Zealand's 4 million people. As with other indigenous groups who did not have a natural immunity to European diseases, three-fourths of the Maoris died in the first decades after European explorers landed. The educational achievement of Maori children also lagged behind their white neighbors. In the 1960s, a Play Centre preschool movement encouraged Maori mothers to use English with their children. In conjunction with the spread of radio and television into Maori homes, this accelerated Maori language loss.

To counter the rapid loss of their language, Maori leaders decided to capitalize on the fact that many elders still spoke their language, and in 1982, they started a Maori immersion preschool movement, called *Te Kohanga Reo*, which translates as "the language nest" and utilizes fluent Maori-speaking elders. The main features of these preschools were that Maori was the only language to be spoken and heard, no smoking was allowed, they were to be kept very clean in the interest of health, and parents and preschool teachers were the decision makers. The preschools spread rapidly, and by 1998, there were more than six hundred. As more and more Maori-speaking children graduated from these preschools, parents who wanted their children's Maori education continued in the public schools put pressure on New Zealand's government to establish Maori immersion elementary schools. Using wording from the 1840 Treaty of Waitangi with the British government, the Maoris were able to convince the government to build on the success of the preschools by providing Maori immersion elementary schools, then secondary schools, and finally Maori language university programs. Timoti Karetu, the former New Zealand Maori Language Commissioner, was so impressed by his visit to Navajo Community College in 1976, that he was largely responsible for establishing Maori immersion teacher preparation at some of New Zealand's universities.

HAWAIIAN PUNANA LEO

Under the Hawaiian monarchy in the nineteenth century, Hawaiians ran their own schools that taught their children to read and write the Hawaiian language. However, after the overthrow of the monarchy in 1893 by American missionaries and colonists, the use of the Hawaiian language was outlawed in schools. The result was that by the 1980s, only a small percentage of Native Hawaiians could still speak their language, and most of these remaining speakers were over fifty years old. Despite not being allowed to speak the Hawaiian language, Native Hawaiian children still did not do well in school.

Native Hawaiians share a common Polynesian ancestry with the Maoris and face the same rapid erosion of their language and lack of academic success in public schools. After visiting the Maoris and witnessing the revitalization of their language, which was largely due to taking ownership of the education of their children, Native Hawaiians started their own family-based immersion preschools in 1984. After parents petitioned the state to change its English-Only law, Hawaiian immersion kindergartens were established in 1987. In 1996, there were 9 sites serving 175 children, and in 2003, there were 12 preschools and 23 public schools with immersion classes. Running typically from 7:30 A.M. to 5:00 P.M., Monday through Thursday, the preschools generally have between ten and thirty children aged three to five. The curriculum is patterned after traditional Hawaiian home life, hula schools, and Sunday schools.

Preschoolers usually enter the *Punana Leo* speaking little or no Hawaiian, but they are not specifically taught Hawaiian, other than to memorize a few phrases, such as asking to receive learning in a traditional chant, formal introductions, and songs. Teachers and older children model the use of Hawaiian to meet the needs of younger children and immerse them in it, so that in six months most of them begin speaking Hawaiian. Although English is not taught in this immersion program, it continues to be taught outside the school. The pervasiveness of English outside the schools has led to students being taught only in Hawaiian up through the fourth grade.

A parent described the *Punana Leo* as "a way of life . . . you have to take it home." He said it was bringing back the moral values of the culture and helping mend families. Parents stay

The *Punana Leo* movement in Hawaii was modeled after similar programs that were established by the Maoris in New Zealand in the early 1980s. Today, there are twelve preschools and twenty-three public schools in Hawaii that have immersion programs. Seen here are students from the Kula Kaiapuni 'O Waiau School on Oahu performing a hula dance.

involved by learning the language and volunteering to help clean the preschool. The mission statement reads:

> The *Punana Leo* Movement grew out of a dream that there be reestablished throughout Hawai'i the mana of a living Hawaiian language from the depth of our origins. The *Punana Leo* initiates, provides for and nurtures various Hawaiian Language environments, and we find our strength in our spirituality, love of our language, love of our people, love of our land, and love of knowledge.[50]

The first immersion students graduated from high school in 1999, and the University of Hawai'i at Hilo has developed a Hawaiian immersion teacher-preparation program in which

Hawaiian language teaching materials are being developed. Immersion programs have helped Native Hawaiian students identify their indigenous identity through academics. The goal of the Hawaiian immersion programs is to reestablish the traditional Hawaiian philosophy of life and apply it to modern times.

Language and Culture Revitalization versus Gangs

Northern Cheyenne educator and tribal college president Dr. Richard Littlebear, speaking at an indigenous language conference in 1997 at Northern Arizona University, described the results of the breakdown of his people's tribal identity and the healing possibilities of tribal language and culture revitalization:

> Our youth are apparently looking to urban gangs for those things that will give them a sense of identity, importance, and belongingness. It would be so nice if they would but look to our own tribal characteristics because we already have all the things that our youth are apparently looking for and finding in socially destructive gangs. We have all the characteristics in our tribal structures that will reaffirm the identities of our youth. Gangs have distinctive colors, clothes, music, heroes, symbols, rituals, and "turf." . . . We American Indian tribes have these too. We have distinctive colors, clothes, music, heroes, symbols, and rituals, and we need to teach our children about the positive aspects of American Indian life at an early age so they know who they are. Perhaps in this way we can inoculate them against the disease of gangs. Another characteristic that really makes a gang distinctive is the language they speak. If we could transfer the young people's loyalty back to our own tribes and families, we could restore the frayed social fabric of our reservations. We need to make our children see our languages and cultures as viable and just as valuable as anything they see on television, movies, or videos.*

* Richard Littlebear, "Some Rare and Radical Ideas for Keeping Indigenous Languages Alive," in *Revitalizing Indigenous Languages*, eds. Jon Reyhner, Gina Cantoni, R.N. St. Clair, and E. Parsons Yazzie (Flagstaff, Ariz.: Northern Arizona University, 1999), 4–5. Available at *http://jan.ucc.nau.edu/~jar/RIL_1.html*.

Challenges to successful language revitalization programs include the pervasiveness of English, the old assimilationist mentality that associated indigenous identity with "savagery," the lack of indigenous language materials to use in schools, and the lack of fluent teachers. However, the commitment of Hawaiian language activists is overcoming these challenges.

THE CREE WAY

The Crees are the largest group of Indians in Canada, and several villages in Quebec have maintained their Cree language. The Waskaganish Crees live in one of eight villages on the eastern shore of James Bay, in northern Quebec. Traditionally hunters and gatherers, the Waskaganish Crees were forced to send their children to federal public schools in the 1960s and were impacted by the building of large hydroelectric dams that brought in outside workers and flooded some of their traditional lands. The introduction of a cash economy disrupted their traditional trapping and hunting economy, as it had previously for other Native Americans throughout North America.

The Cree Way project was created in 1973 by a school principal to counteract the Canadian curriculum being used to educate Cree children. Its purpose was to bridge the enormous gap between the tribal Crees and urban Euro-Canadians and to validate Cree culture and tribal identity. In addition to supporting the traditional oral culture, the project also sought to promote literacy. Although a Cree syllabary (a writing system using symbols to represent syllables) was developed more than a century ago, there were no schoolbooks that used the syllabary, and Crees did not use it in everyday life. The Cree Way project began developing Cree language materials and teaching Cree to students. There are now more than five hundred textbooks in Cree.

The problem with early programs like Cree Way was that Cree was taught like a foreign language for a half hour or so a day, which is not enough for most students to be able to speak or read it well. A Cree preschool immersion program was started in 1988 in order to allow students more time to learn Cree, and it was expanded to include kindergarten through fourth grade over the years that followed. Fourth grade was taught half in Cree and half in either French or English. As was the case at Rock Point Community School on the Navajo Reservation in Arizona, students took Cree enrichment courses from fifth grade through high school.

The Cree Way program supports the transmission of important cultural experiences through bush camps and a rescheduling of summer vacation so that students have a week in the fall and three weeks in the spring for hunting and ceremonies with their elders and families. At the bush camps, which are held four or five times a year, students are taught the skills of trapping, beading, snowshoe construction, cooking, and hide tanning. Students write in Cree in their journals about their camp experiences.

In 1970, the Province of Quebec recognized the right of Native peoples to have their language taught in public schools. The French-speaking majority in Quebec was especially sensitive to the issue of language rights, because they were surrounded by the English-speaking Canadian majority. In the early 1970s, there was no avenue for Crees to become certified teachers. To remedy this problem the University of Quebec began a teacher-preparation program that was then continued by McGill University. The 1975 James Bay Agreement placed authority for schools directly in tribal hands. Each community elected a school board to hire staff and oversee language policy, curriculum, and textbook approval; as a result, in the 1990s, 50 percent of the teaching staff were Crees. Local school boards provided workshops to develop culturally relevant curriculum using local teachers. This new curriculum reduced the high drop-out rate, and most graduates who went on for university training returned to their home villages. Many junior and senior high students choose to take French as a third language.

THE PEACH SPRINGS HUALAPAIS

An example of a small tribe in the United States working to maintain its language is the Hualapai, which translates as "the people of the tall pines." Their reservation is located on the south rim of the Grand Canyon in Arizona. In 1994, there were seventeen hundred Hualapais and almost half were below the age of sixteen. Traditionally the Hualapais were hunter-gatherers and subsistence farmers who lived in small bands with a headman as leader. The U.S. government established a reservation for them in 1883, and an elected tribal government headquartered in the village of Peach Springs, Arizona, was set up as well.

In the mid-1970s, almost half of the two hundred students at the Peach Springs public school spoke predominantly English and the establishment of government housing weakened traditional extended families by separating them into individual houses. A bilingual program was started in the school in an attempt to stop the rapid loss of the Hualapai language, and a writing system was developed and used for new curriculum materials. However, bilingual programs in schools have not proven to be able to halt the loss of Native language. By the early 1980s, more than 90 percent of students came from homes in which only elders still spoke Hualapai and the children spoke English.

A parallel Hualapai curriculum was developed to complement the English curriculum, which balanced the use of the two languages in order for one language to reinforce what was being learned in the other language. This curriculum utilized computers, and included a video studio and television station, where students produced and scripted Hualapai documentaries for use in classrooms and the community. In addition, much of the language arts program was computerized.

CONCLUSION

Just as it proved impossible for non-Native Americans to wipe out Native American languages by demanding assimilation, Native American languages cannot be revitalized by non-Native Americans, though they can be helped by culturally sensitive linguists and others. Successful language revitalization efforts are dependent on family and community support. Children need to hear and speak their mother tongue when they are very young. Ideally, this exposure begins in the home, but immersion preschools like those pioneered by the Maoris and Hawaiians can be very effective.

English and other international languages are very powerful, and unless indigenous peoples can work together locally and internationally, their languages will be forgotten. Indigenous communities cannot afford to fight over dialectical

The Importance of Learning Outside the Classroom

Having well-prepared teachers doing a good job of instructing in the classroom is not enough to guarantee students' success. Children need to use what they learn outside the classroom, whether it is language or any other subject. There is an old saying, "Use it or lose [forget] it." Gary Owens, an education specialist with the Salt River Pima-Maricopa Indian Community O'Odham-Piipassh Language Program, writes:

There needs to be freedom to use the language *inside* the schools. Take it outside of that curriculum and set it free to run and scamper all over the place. Take it away from the lesson plans, the worksheets, and please . . . do not have the gall to test our children on what they know in regards to learning the language. Instead create a place where they can show you what they have learned.*

* Gary Owens, Meld k e'esto ge al'aliga, in *Nurturing Native Languages*, eds. Jon Reyhner, Octaviana Trujillo, R.L. Carrasco, and Louise Lockard (Flagstaff, Ariz.: Northern Arizona University, 2003), xi. Available at *http://jan.ucc.nau.edu/~jar/NNL/NNL_Owens.pdf*.

differences in their languages or whether or not their languages should be written down.

Parents need to be convinced that indigenous language programs will not hurt their children's chance to get a good education and find good jobs. This is challenging because to successfully revitalize an indigenous language, children need to be immersed in it for an extended period of time. Immersion takes more than simply finding someone who speaks a language and having them speak it all the time with their students. Immersion teachers need preparation, and one reason English Only campaigns have been successful in getting antibilingual education legislation passed is that not all bilingual education programs have been equal to the one at Rock Point. When bilingual programs were started after the passage of the Bilingual Education Act in 1968, there was a lack of trained teachers and administrators. When teachers lack training, their students will not learn to speak fluently. They simply learn vocabulary, such as the names of colors, animals, and numbers.

Since 1968, universities have been working to hire professors who can prepare teachers to teach bilingually. For example, the American Indian Language Development Institute (AILDI), at the University of Arizona, has been offering summer training since 1978 for teachers and others interested in revitalizing Native American languages. In Canada, there is now a similar Canadian Indigenous Languages and Literacy Development Institute (CILLDI), which was founded in 1999. Indigenous language immersion is in its infancy in the continental United States; though there are some successful programs, such as the Arapaho language immersion program on the Wind River Reservation in Wyoming and the Blackfeet immersion program in Montana, the majority are relegated mainly to small preschools.

5

Language Policies and Education Goals

In the 1980s, Indian tribes exercised their self-determination in many areas. A few of them examined bilingual education and Native language revitalization. In 1984, the Navajo Tribal Council passed Navajo Tribal Education Policies. In the preface to the policies, Navajo Tribal Chairman Peterson Zah wrote: "We believe that an excellent education can produce achievement in the basic academic skills and skills required by modern technology and still educate young Navajo citizens in their language, history, government and culture." The policies required schools serving Navajo students to offer courses in Navajo history and culture, and supported local control, parental involvement, Native American preference in hiring, and instruction in the Navajo language. The council declared:

> The Navajo language is an essential element of the life, culture and

identity of the Navajo people. The Navajo Nation recognizes the importance of preserving and perpetuating that language to the survival of the Nation. Instruction in the Navajo language shall be made available for all grade levels in all schools serving the Navajo Nation. Navajo language instruction shall include to the greatest extent practicable: thinking, speaking, comprehension, reading and writing skills and study of the formal grammar of the language.[51]

A year later the Northern Ute Tribal Business Committee approved a resolution declaring:

The Ute language is the official language of the Northern Ute Nation and may be used in the business of government—legislative, executive and judicial—although in deference to, and out of respect to speakers of English, English may be utilized in official matters of government.

We declare that the Ute language is a living and vital language that has the ability to match any other in the world for expressiveness and beauty. Our language is capable of lexical expansion into modern conceptual fields such as the field of politics, economics, mathematics and science.

Be it known that the Ute language shall be recognized as our first language, and the English language will be recognized as our second language. We assert that our students are fully capable of developing fluency in our mother tongue and the foreign English language and we further assert that a higher level of Ute mastery results in higher levels of English skills.[52]

The Northern Ute Tribe required Ute language instruction for preschool through twelfth grade, encouraged "pre-service training in Ute language theory and methodology for teachers," and required three credits of in-service training in Ute language for teachers within one year of employment.

In the 1980s, tribes such as the Navajo and Ute passed resolutions to have their children taught the history, culture, and language of their people in the classroom. Shortly thereafter, the Native American Languages Act was signed into law by President George H.W. Bush in October 1990, calling for Native American culture and language to be protected both in schools and governing bodies. Shown here is a student at the Ojibwe Immersion School, on the Lac Courte Oreilles Chippewa Reservation, Hayward, Wisconsin.

NATIVE AMERICAN LANGUAGES ACT OF 1990

After getting their own state anti-Hawaiian language bill revoked, Hawaiian language activists worked to get the U.S. government to renounce its past assimilationist policies against Native languages. The work of conservative organizations such as U.S. English and English First to get a constitutional amendment to make English the official language of the United States was especially worrisome to the Hawaiians, Navajos, Utes, and others working to revive their languages. With the support of World War II veteran and Hawaii senator Daniel K. Inouye, they were finally successful. On October 30, 1990, President George H.W. Bush signed the Native American Languages Act. In this law, Congress declared "the status of the cultures and languages of Native Americans is unique and the United States has the responsibility to act together with Native Americans to ensure the survival of these unique cultures and languages." The act made it a federal law to "preserve, protect, and promote the rights and freedom of Native Americans to use, practice, and develop Native American languages. . . . The right of Indian tribes and other Native American governing bodies to use the Native American languages as a medium of instruction in all schools funded by the Secretary of the Interior" was also recognized. It declared that "the right of Native Americans to express themselves through the use of Native American languages shall not be restricted in any public proceeding, including publicly supported education programs."[53]

INDIAN NATIONS AT RISK TASK FORCE

Language revitalization was just one of the concerns of Native peoples in regard to the education of their children. In 1986, under the leadership of Secretary of Education Terrel H. Bell, the U.S. Department of Education issued a report titled *A Nation at Risk* that received wide publicity. The report criticized the education American children were receiving in schools and called for the strengthening of America's public schools. Native American leaders, well aware of the high drop-out rates for their children, lobbied to get a similar study that focused on Native American children. In 1990, U.S. Secretary of Education Lauro Cavazos chartered an Indian Nations at Risk (INAR) Task Force that issued a report the following year titled *Indian Nations at Risk: An Educational Strategy for Action*. The task force gathered testimony at regional public hearings and at the annual conference of the National Indian Education Association, made thirty school-site visits, and commissioned twenty-one papers from national experts on Native American/Alaska Native education

on current conditions, funding, drop-out prevention, curriculum, and related issues.

In its report, the task force's cochairs, former Secretary of
Education Terrel H. Bell and former Alaska Commissioner of
Education William G. Demmert, Jr. (Tlingit/Sioux), wrote:

> The Task Force believes that a well-educated American
> Indian and Alaska Native citizenry and a renewal of the lan-
> guage and culture base of the American Native community
> will strengthen self-determination and economic well-being
> and will allow the Native community to contribute to build-
> ing a stronger nation—an America that can compete with
> other nations and contribute to the world's economies and
> cultures.[54]

The cochairs identified four reasons that Indian
Nations are at risk:

1) Schools have failed to educate large numbers of
   Indian students and adults . . . [as indicated by]
   high drop-out rates and negative attitudes toward
   school;
2) Schools have discouraged the use of Native languages . . . [with the result that] the language and
   culture base of the American Native are rapidly
   eroding;
3) The diminished lands and natural resources of the
   American Native are constantly under siege; and
4) Indian self-determination and governance rights
   are challenged by the changing policies of the
   administration, Congress, and the justice system.[55]

The Task Force reported that during the 1989–1990 school
year, 39,791 Native students (10 percent of the total) were
attending 166 Bureau of Indian Affairs (BIA)-funded schools,
9,743 (3 percent) were attending private schools, and 333,494

(87 percent) were attending public schools. Testimony gathered at the task force hearings indicated that many Native students were attending schools with "an unfriendly school climate that fails to promote appropriate academic, social, cultural, and spiritual development among many Native students." Schools also had a Euro-centric curriculum, low teacher expectations, "a lack of Native educators as role models," and "overt and subtle racism." These factors contributed to Native students having the highest high school drop-out rate (36 percent) of any minority group in the United States.

In a more positive light, the task force learned:

> . . . there is a direct relationship between students' understanding of their culture and role in society and their ability to function comfortably in society and to achieve academic success. When students' relationships with the larger society are strained, their chances for academic success appear to diminish . . . .
>
> Often schools have failed to make clear to students the connection between what they learn in school and what they must know to live comfortably and contribute to society.[56]

The task force called for "establishing the promotion of students' tribal language and culture as a responsibility of the school" and "training of Native teachers to increase the number of Indian educators and other professionals." Furthermore, they recommended that school officials and educators "integrate the contemporary, historical, and cultural perspectives of American Indians" and "give education a multicultural focus to eliminate racism and promote understanding among all races."

State governments were encouraged to provide funding "to develop and use linguistically, culturally, and developmentally appropriate curricula" for Native American students, and the federal government was asked to "fund more research on Indian education." Colleges and universities were encouraged to "do more scholarly work on curricula and textbook development that incorporates Native perspectives."

Overall, the task force's report strongly supported the need for culturally appropriate education for Native American and Alaska Native students and echoed the Native American Languages Act in calling for the maintenance of Native languages and cultures in schools. At the task force hearings held

Indian Nations at Risk Task Force Goals for Native American Education

Using President George H.W. Bush's six National Education Goals as a guideline, the Indian Nations at Risk Task Force established a set of their own education goals in 1991 to facilitate the improvement of all federal, tribal, private, and public schools that serve Native Americans and Alaska Natives and their communities. The task force originally set out to meet the following goals by the year 2000, and Native Americans are still focusing on these areas in the hope of helping their children achieve success in the classroom.

GOAL 1: Readiness for School—All Native children will have access to early childhood education programs that provide the language, social, physical, spiritual, and cultural foundations they need to succeed in school and to reach their full potential as adults.

GOAL 2: Maintain Native Languages and Cultures—All schools will offer Native students the opportunity to maintain and develop their tribal languages and will create a multicultural environment that enhances the many cultures represented in the school.

GOAL 3: Literacy—All Native children in school will be literate in the language skills appropriate for their individual levels of development. They will be competent in their English oral, reading, listening, and writing skills.

GOAL 4: Student Academic Achievement—Every Native student will demonstrate mastery of English, mathematics, science, history, geography, and other challenging academic skills necessary for an educated citizenry.

GOAL 5: High School Graduation—All Native students capable of completing high school will graduate. They will demonstrate civic, social, creative, and across the country in 1990 and 1991, parents, tribal leaders, and educators emphasized the need for the cultural revitalization of Native communities to fight problems of drug and alcohol abuse, unemployment, and dysfunctional families. Repeated testimony focused on the need for more Native community involvement in Native education. Too often parents were only asked to be "cake bakers and cops"—to help with

critical thinking skills necessary for ethical, moral, and responsible citizenship and important in modern tribal, national, and world societies.

GOAL 6: *High-Quality Native and non-Native School Personnel*—The numbers of Native educators will double, and the colleges and universities that train the nation's teachers will develop a curriculum that prepares teachers to work effectively with a variety of cultures, including the Native cultures that are served by schools.

GOAL 7: *Safe and Alcohol-Free and Drug-Free Schools*—Every school responsible for educating Native students will be free of alcohol and drugs and will provide safe facilities and an environment conducive to learning.

GOAL 8: *Adult Education and Lifelong Learning*—Every Native adult will have the opportunity to be literate and to obtain the necessary academic, vocational, and technical skills and knowledge needed to gain meaningful employment and to exercise the rights and responsibilities of tribal and national citizenship.

GOAL 9: *Restructuring Schools*—Schools serving Native children will be restructured to effectively meet the academic, cultural, spiritual, and social needs of students for developing strong, healthy, self-sufficient communities.

GOAL 10: *Parental, Community, and Tribal Partnerships*—Every school responsible for educating Native students will provide opportunities for Native parents and tribal leaders to help plan and evaluate the governance, operation, and performance of their educational programs.*

* Indian Nations at Risk Task Force. *Indian Nations at Risk: An Educational Strategy for Action* (Final report of the Indian Nations at Risk Task Force) (U.S. Department of Education Washington, D.C., October 1991).

school fund-raising and to get their kids to school on time. Until Native communities felt a sense of ownership in their schools, Native education would continue to be an unsuccessful colonial enterprise. In addition, testimony was heard that racism was still alive and well in the United States and was hurting Native children.

WHITE HOUSE CONFERENCE ON INDIAN EDUCATION

Another federal initiative that was focused on improving Native American education was the White House conference that took place in Washington, D.C., in 1992. It was authorized by Congress to "explore the feasibility of establishing an independent Board of Indian Education that would assume responsibility for all existing federal programs relating to the education of Indians" and "to develop recommendations for the improvement of educational programs relevant to the needs of Indians." Two hundred and thirty-four conference delegates were chosen from across the United States to discuss ways to improve Native education. They included teachers, school administrators, tribal leaders, and government officials.

In states with large Native American populations, preconferences were held to discuss whether there should be a national board of Native American education, a national Native American university, and what should be the national goals of Native American education. Much of the discussion at these preconferences echoed the concerns expressed at the INAR hearings. The New Mexico preconference delegates reported:

> When the idea of the White House Conference was first presented to us, there was much negativity and frustration expressed because it was thought of as another federal project that would collect the information, publish a report and place it on a shelf in Washington.[57]

Their report also stated:

> In reference to the quality and training of teachers, confer-
> ence participants felt that some teachers are currently
> employed in the public schools primarily on the basis of
> their certification, with little consideration given to other
> important factors that directly affect the education of Indian
> children. Improved training and selection of teachers for
> public schools serving predominantly Indian populations
> was identified as a continuing need. In addition, the cur-
> riculum content found in most public schools was charac-
> terized as having been developed for mainstream America,
> without regard for cultural differences. Participants stressed
> the importance of enhancing the basic curriculum through
> the inclusion of local culture, history and language and that
> Native American parents and tribal leaders assist in the
> development of these curricula.[58]

Building on the work of the state preconferences and the
Indian Nations at Risk Task Force, the White House Conference
delegates adopted 113 resolutions covering a variety of topics,
ranging from the governance of Native American education to
safe, alcohol-/drug-free schools.

Although the continued conservative backlash to the Civil
Rights movement prevented any major legislation from being
passed based on the findings of the task force's report or the
White House Conference on Indian Education, progress was,
nonetheless, being made. For example, publishers worked to
include more content about and pictures of minorities in their
textbooks. Sometimes this amounted to a token "sunburning";
coloring an illustration of a white person or making Robert
Roberto. One interesting change was the renaming of Custer
Battlefield National Monument in Montana to the Little
Bighorn Battlefield National Monument. Because U.S.
Lieutenant Colonel George Armstrong Custer was defeated by
the combined forces of the Cheyenne and Sioux, it did not

In December 1991, Congress passed legislation that approved the renaming of Custer Battlefield National Monument and set up memorials—which were built in 1999 and 2001—to honor the Sioux and Cheyennes who died at the Battle of the Little Bighorn in June 1876. Here, several Native Americans venerate their relatives by participating in a tribal song in recognition of the name change to Little Bighorn Battlefield National Monument.

make a lot of sense to name the battlefield after him, and when the National Park Service named a Native American as superintendent of the monument, she was able, with congressional help, to get the name changed.

After the White House Conference, the federal government showed little further interest in Native American education until President William Clinton issued an Executive Order in 1998 on American Indian and Alaska Native Education that set six goals: improving reading and mathematics scores; increasing high school completion and postsecondary attendance rates; reducing the influence of long-standing factors that impede educational performance, such as poverty and substance abuse; creating strong, safe, and drug-free school environments; improving science education; and expanding the use of educational technology.

The need to improve American Indian and Alaska Native student achievement was highlighted by a 2001 General Accounting Office study that found "their performance on standardized tests and other measures is far below the performance of students in public schools"; even though in 1999, the 171 BIA-funded schools that served 47,080 students generally spent more per pupil than public schools. The study found that 17 percent of BIA students still resided in school dormitories. Although most BIA schools were in the states of Arizona, New Mexico, North and South Dakota, and Washington, there were also schools in Maine, Florida, and many other states. For the 2000–2001 school year, the BIA's Office of Indian Education Programs reported there were 65 schools directly operated by the BIA and 120 schools operated by tribes in 23 states. These schools had an average daily attendance rate of 90 percent.[59]

On January 8, 2002, President George W. Bush signed the No Child Left Behind Act of 2001. This Act states:

> It is the policy of the United States to fulfill the Federal Government's unique and continuing trust relationship with and responsibility to the Indian people for the education of Indian children. The Federal Government will continue to work with local educational agencies, Indian tribes and organizations, postsecondary institutions, and other entities toward the goal of ensuring that programs that serve Indian children are of the highest quality and provide for not only the basic elementary and secondary educational needs, but also the unique educational and culturally related academic needs of these children.[60]

This act contained extensive provisions to insure educational accountability for Native American and other students, with critics labeling it the "No Child Left Untested Act." The critics are concerned that Native American and other minority students must pass high-stakes tests to be promoted to the next grade or graduate, with the result that more would drop out of school. Many consider these one-size-fits-all tests inappropriate for Native American and other minority students. The tests are made up of questions that legislators and other policy makers think is appropriate for mainstream American students.

A heated controversy continues between liberals and conservatives on how best to educate students in general, and Native American and other minority children in particular. The next two chapters address various aspects of this controversy.

6

Language Teaching

THE BILINGUAL VERSUS MONOLINGUAL DEBATE

The United States is rather unique in the world as a country where most of the population is monolingual, speaking only one language. In most of the world, bilingualism is common and one can find many people also speaking three or more languages. Despite the fact that speaking two languages (being bilingual) is common worldwide, in the United States there is a strong movement against bilingual education, or the teaching of two languages in schools. The common perception of many people who have not studied the subject is that any teaching of a non-English language in schools will mean the students will learn less English. Bilingualism has also been considered by some to be a handicap because it was thought that people would confuse the two languages they spoke, but research indicates such confusion is at most a temporary condition. A third reason for opposing bilingual education is that it will divide loyalties.

In the United States, there has been a strong movement toward making English the official language; twenty-one of the twenty-seven states that recognize English as the official language have passed English-first legislation since 1981. However, the instruction of Native languages has gained support in recent years and is now being taught in many tribal schools. Here, a tribal elder teaches the Walla Walla language to a student on the Umatilla Indian Reservation in Oregon.

People supporting making English the official language see its dominance threatened by immigrants and consider it the "glue" that holds our country together and a cure-all to the problems of poverty faced by many ethnic minorities in the United States. Already, more than half the states have some kind of official English law. Louisiana's 1811 law is the oldest of these, and Iowa's 2002 law is the most recent. This concern over the importance of English is comparatively recent. Twenty-one of the twenty-seven states with Official English laws have passed them since 1981.

A letter to the editor in the December 27, 1999, issue of

USA Today claimed, "The one thing that binds the USA as a nation and makes possible the blending of so many varied cultural and ethnic mixes is that we have a common language." A similar letter appeared in the November 21, 2000, issue of the *Arizona Republic*. Its author insisted, "We must all be able to communicate in one language, the only glue uniting this great country." Others maintain that the "glue" holding this country together is not the English language but rather the ideas embodied in the Declaration of Independence, the U.S. Constitution, and other key documents of the democratic experience; ideas that can be lived and expressed eloquently in languages other than English. The definitions of *freedom, liberty*, and *justice for all* in those documents need to be broadened to include group as well as individual rights to heritage, languages, and cultures.

Government suppression of minority languages and cultures violates the liberty of Native American, Latino, and other language minority citizens. Forced conformity is still being imposed on ethnic minorities in the United States through assimilationist, English-only schooling to the detriment of full and equal citizenship. Research indicates that immigrants are learning English faster now than ever before; thus, the dominance of English in the United States is in no way threatened. On the contrary, immigrant languages are threatened. In the words of attorney Lani Guinier and others, minorities are being subjected to democracy's "tyranny of the majority." Native Americans, who comprise roughly 1 percent of the nation's population, are defenseless in the face of the majority unless they present a united front, link arms with other minorities, and actively recruit the support of mainstream Americans. In his 2000 book, *Democracy Derailed: Initiative Campaigns and the Power of Money*, journalist David Broder details how the initiative process in California and other states can submerge minority viewpoints and offer slogan-driven cure-alls to deep-rooted societal problems.

It is unjust to consider bilingualism un-American and a handicap for minorities and the poor, while at the other end of the spectrum, bilingualism is considered a sign of a truly educated person among the rich. Prestigious universities like Harvard, Northwestern, and Stanford often require new students to have taken two or more years of a foreign language in high school, and usually require their students to take several more language courses to graduate. Research has shown that people who speak two languages fluently are smarter than people who speak only one language. For example, someone who speaks only one language can confuse a word with what that word stands for. People who are bilingual are more aware that words in their language are just labels and not to be confused with the thing, idea, etc., that the word stands for.

Although university language requirements are important, they do not guarantee that students who take a second language in high school or college will be able to speak the language fluently. There are stories of students who have taken four years of French in high school who go to Paris and cannot carry on a conversation in French.

METHODS OF INSTRUCTION

Older methods of teaching languages focused on the grammar of a language and translating one language to the other, rather than carrying on a conversation. With the grammar translation method, students learned to conjugate verbs in the present, past, and future tenses in the first, second, and third person, but that is not the same as carrying on a conversation.

In nineteenth-century Native American boarding schools, teachers emphasized an "object method" of teaching a language. For example, Don Talayesva, a Hopi, described his first experience at a BIA school in 1899 in his autobiography, *Sun Chief*:

> The first thing I learned in school was "nail," a hard word to remember. Every day when we entered the classroom a nail

lay on the desk. The teacher would take it up and say, "What is this?" Finally I answered "nail" ahead of the other boys and was called "bright."[61]

Another Hopi, Helen Sekaquaptewa, who attended the Keams Canyon Boarding School in the first decade of the twentieth century, remembered a similar experience. She recalled in her autobiography, *My and Mine*, "Our teacher was Miss Stanley. She began by teaching us the names of objects about the room. We read a little from big charts on the wall later on, but I don't remember ever using any books."[62] John Fire, a Lakota born around 1903, recalled one of his teachers used objects: She would "hold up one stick and say, 'One.' Then she'd hold up two sticks and say, 'Two,' over and over again. For many weeks she showed us pictures of animals and said 'dog' or 'cat.' It took me three years to learn to say 'I want this.'" He recalled spending six years in third grade, which was as high as his neighborhood school went, and that "in all those years at the day school they never taught me to speak English or to write and read. I learned these things only many years later, in saloons, in the Army or in jail."[63]

One of the dangers of learning a new language or learning to read is that one will memorize language and repeat it from memory. This is called "parroting" because that is how parrots "talk." In his 1928 book, *My People the Sioux*, Luther Standing Bear complained that his students did better than the students of white teachers who got all their knowledge from books "but outside of that, they knew nothing." He wrote:

> The Indian children should have been taught how to translate the Sioux tongue into English properly; but the English teachers only taught them the English language, like a bunch of parrots. While they could read all the words placed before them, they did not know the proper use of them; their meaning was a puzzle.[64]

When schools started using tape recorders in the 1960s, a language teaching method called the audiolingual approach was used. Students would go to a language lab and listen to taped conversations in the language they were trying to learn. However, memorizing these prerecorded conversations was similar to the parroting Luther Standing Bear described and not the equivalent of being able to carry on a conversation about some new topic.

Immersion

One of the best ways to learn a language is to move to where the

Learning That Immersion Works by Accident

More than a century ago, a language teacher named Maximilian Delphinius Berlitz got sick in Providence, Rhode Island, and had to hire a substitute teacher. It turned out that his substitute, who could not speak English, did a better job of teaching French than Berlitz. This led to the development of the Berlitz language schools, which use an immersion teaching method in which students are taught without translation. The Berlitz method is based on a series of statements and questions that involve three objects, statements, or situations. The real or realistic content of the questions keeps the students focused, and the use of three different objects keeps the students from parroting responses. The learning cycle begins with three statements that in the beginning may focus on three simple, real objects; for example, a piece of paper, a pencil, and a book. The questioning then rotates from negative to positive responses and then back to statements (Pencil? No. Book? No. Paper? Yes.). In short order, the cycle of statements and questions becomes quite complex: Is Tom going to New York? No. Tom is not going to New York. Is Tom going to Toronto? No. Mr. Berlitz is not going to Toronto. Where is Tom going? Tom is going to San Francisco. . . . Is Jane going to San Francisco? No. . . . Is Jane going to New York? And so forth. Consequently, in a Berlitz language lesson, the teacher models the target language half the time by asking questions. The students spend the other half of the class answering the questions in the target language.

language is spoken and immerse oneself in that language. Immersion teaching methods have shown a marked improvement over earlier language teaching approaches, such as the older grammar translation and audiolingual methods. The central characteristic of immersion is the teaching of language, content, and culture in combination—without the use of the child's first language. Students are taught a second language they initially do not understand, through the use of a variety of context clues provided by the teacher.

The first extensive research on immersion teaching occurred in Quebec. At the same time the Civil Rights movement was gaining strength in the United States, the French-speaking people in Canada, who mainly live in the Province of Quebec, began to protest their second-class status as citizens and started an independence movement. Because they represent a majority of the people in Quebec, French speakers were able to pass laws requiring the use of the French language. English-speaking parents living in the suburbs of Montreal, Quebec, came to the conclusion that their children would have no future in a French-speaking Quebec unless they learned French. However, they knew that having their children take French classes in high school would not be enough to enable their children to read, write, and speak fluent French. These parents went to university professors and asked them the best way to help their children to become fluent French/English bilinguals. The professors suggested setting up immersion schools that began teaching these English-speaking children French from kindergarten through third grade. Around fourth grade, English was brought back, and it was found in these experimental schools that the students could learn to speak, read, and write French well without hurting their English language abilities.

Immersion language teachers generally provide at least half-day (partial) immersion for students in the language they are targeted to learn and often students receive full-day (total) immersion. The less students are exposed to a new language they are learning outside of school, the more they need to be exposed to it in school. Children will learn to speak a high-prestige language, such as English, that is omnipresent in their community and in the media, even if it receives no support in the school; however, they will need instruction to use it for school work.

Since the success of French immersion programs in Quebec, the programs have become increasingly popular. Test scores show that immersion students can learn the same academic content as students in English Only classrooms, along with a second language, without losing fluency in English. As immersion students proceed together through school, they also develop a strong sense of camaraderie and often form a "values community" that reflects the positive aspects of the language and culture they are learning.

One unintended consequence of the success of the French immersion programs was that, during Ronald Reagan's presidency, they were mistakenly viewed as a model for Spanish-speaking students in the United States. Although the French immersion programs were additive in that they were intended to produce students who were fluent in both French and English, these programs took on a different role in the United States—they were implemented to be subtractive and assimilative, replacing Spanish fluency with English fluency. Additive bilingual programs are not intended to attack students' identity and do not produce all the negative consequences that such attacks may cause. However, subtractive programs can have all the bad effects of other assimilationist approaches to education, which attempt to replace one culture with another.

Total Physical Response

A popular immersion approach for beginning language learners is Total Physical Response (TPR), which was popularized in the

1970s by psychologist James J. Asher. TPR begins with a "silent period" in which learners respond physically to simple requests by the teacher, who uses gestures to help communicate to the students what the teacher wants them to do. The acting out of the requested behaviors help students remember the meaning of the new phrases they are hearing. Although students initially respond silently to the teacher's requests, after just a few lessons, they are soon asking other students to perform actions, including recombining vocabulary that the teacher has been using and making requests that they have never heard before.

In TPR, students are first asked to "stand up," "walk," and "jump," and in advanced TPR, students act out skits. Indian language revitalization activists like Northern Cheyenne Richard Littlebear and Ho Chunk (also known as Winnebago) Preston Thompson have found TPR an effective way to teach their languages. TPR, however, is not really a new technique. John Fire (Lakota Sioux) recalled his early-twentieth-century day school experiences on the Rosebud Reservation in his autobiography, *Lame Deer: Seeker of Visions*. His teacher told him "'Stand,' 'sit down'! . . . again and again until we caught on. 'Sit, stand, sit, stand. Go and stop. Yes and no.' All without spelling, just by sound."[65]

The Natural Approach

The best way to acquire a second language is the same way children acquire a first language: Immerse students in a second language-rich environment rather than the traditional teaching-learning situation. As linguist Judith Lindfors has stated, "What's good for the first-language learner is good for the second." A well-worked-out approach to immersion education is described by Stephen Krashen and Tracy Terrell in their 1984 book, *The Natural Approach*. A list of teacher suggestions adapted from the book includes:

- The teacher almost always uses the language he or she is teaching (this is called "immersion").
- Lessons (what is talked about) should focus on topics of interest and relevancy to the students.
- Lessons should focus on an activity the students perform rather than on grammar.
- The teacher always works to help students understand using gestures, visual aides, and objects.
- The teacher's goal is to get the students to be able to carry on a conversation in the language they are learning (rather than reading a book in it).
- The teacher works to lessen student anxiety by creating a warm, friendly, welcoming classroom and encourages "them to express their ideas, opinions, desires, emotions, and feelings."

Students learn new languages in stages, beginning with a "silent period" in which they only listen to the teacher and do not speak. Then they start speaking single words like "yes" and "no," then a few words, then phrases, and finally they move to sentences. Whatever the method of instruction, learning a language takes time. University of California linguist Leanne Hinton estimates it takes about five hundred hours of practice with listening and speaking to achieve a basic conversational proficiency in a new language.

In the *The Natural Approach*, teachers are advised not to correct errors in grammar and pronunciation that do not interfere with understanding. However, it has been found in Quebec that when these errors are not corrected they can become permanent. Although the students can speak, read, and write French, they do it with accents and grammatical errors.

Although *The Natural Approach* focuses on getting students to the point where they can carry on a conversation in the language they are learning, teachers can focus on topics of interest such as hands-on science and math lessons and develop

The Piegan Institute's Cut-Bank Language Immersion School, on the Blackfeet Reservation in northwestern Montana, is an example of a language immersion school that is focusing on increasing the number of Blackfeet speakers, as well as preserving the tribe's culture and promoting positive change in the community. Here, a student learns the Blackfeet translation for some common English words.

students' academic as well as conversational language proficiency using immersion teaching methods. Math and science are typical content subjects taught through immersion during the primary grades; they are best taught through the use of objects and hands-on activities as described at Rock Point Community School in chapter 2. In higher grades, less time is often spent on second-language immersion and the subject taught is often tribal history and government, because of the difficulty of obtaining appropriate curriculum for other subjects, and the need to develop English, as well as the mother tongue.

Indigenous Language Immersion

Indigenous mother tongue immersion programs are voluntary and require parent involvement. In Hawai'i, parents are required to help in the preschools eight hours per month and to take classes in Hawaiian so they can support the instruction given in the schools. A nonprofit corporation supports the preschools, provides postsecondary scholarships for the study of Hawaiian, and develops Hawaiian language curriculum and materials for use in the schools. Indigenous mother tongue immersion and foreign-or second-language immersion differ in their commitment to culturally transforming the student. Mother tongue immersion seeks to transmit the children's indigenous culture, while foreign-language immersion seeks to create an understanding and appreciation of the culture of the new language.

An example of a small experimental indigenous language immersion school on the Blackfeet Reservation in Montana is the Cut-Bank Language Immersion School, which teaches the Blackfeet language. From his experiences as the school's cofounder, Darrell R. Kipp offers the following advice to people interested in revitalizing their languages:

- *Rule 1*: Never Ask Permission, Never Beg to Save the Language. Go ahead and get started, don't wait even five minutes. Don't wait for a grant . . .
- *Rule 2*: Don't Debate the Issues
- *Rule 3*: Be Very Action-Oriented: Just Act
- *Rule 4*: Show, Don't Tell. Don't talk about what you will do. Do it and show it.[66]

The rapid decline in number of speakers and the importance of language to identity demands the immediate action that Kipp has recommended.

The Importance of Native Languages

In her 1995 doctoral dissertation, *A Study of Reasons for Navajo Language Attrition as Perceived by Navajo Speaking Parents*, Evangeline Parsons Yazzie interviewed Navajos about their language. Their responses included the following: "Truly, it is through our language that safety is reached" and

> When learning Navajo, children are just learning nouns without verbs or without the whole sentence, because of it children don't think too deep, their minds cannot grasp difficult concepts. . . . Culture can only be taught in Navajo; without language, knowledge cannot be transmitted.

Another Navajo told her:

> You are asking questions about the reasons that we are moving out of our language, I know the reason. The television is robbing our children of language . . . It is not only at school that there are teachings, teachings are around us and from us there are also teachings. Our children should not sit around the television. Those who are mothers and fathers should have held their children close to themselves and taught them well, then our grandchildren would have picked up our language.

Parsons Yazzie found in her research that "Elder Navajos want to pass on their knowledge and wisdom to the younger generation. Originally, this was the older people's responsibility. Today the younger generation does not know the language and is unable to accept the words of wisdom." She continues, "The use of the native tongue is like therapy, specific native words express love and caring. . . . Knowing the language presents one with a strong self-identity, a culture with which to identify, and a sense of wellness."

In his 1994 doctoral dissertation, *An Ethnographic Study of Cheyenne Elders: Contributions to Language and Cultural Survival*, Dr. Richard Littlebear (Ve'kesohnestooe) quotes an elder who even more directly voiced the connection of language to identity: "Cheyenne language is us; it is who we are; we talk it, we live it. We are it and it is us."

Cautions

There are many ways that people can argue about how languages should be revitalized. Any of these arguments can damage language revitalization efforts. One controversial topic is when English (or Spanish or French) should be introduced into the curriculum. If students come to school knowing only English, then more time needs to be devoted to indigenous language in school, as is the case with the Maori and Hawaiian immersion programs. However, if students come to school already speaking their indigenous language, as was the case at Rock Point, then they can start learning one of the international languages, such as English, from the start.

One needs to be pragmatic and observe how the program is working and make changes to fit the situation. If parents are worried their children will not be able to get jobs if too much time is devoted to the instruction of indigenous language, those worries have to be recognized and addressed.

Another problem is that of language dialects. Just as English is spoken differently in the South, Northeast, Midwest, and West, indigenous languages can vary from one village to another and from one side of an Indian reservation to another. Ethnocentrism leads speakers to believe that their particular dialect is correct, while other ways are wrong. However, as explained in chapter 1, cultural relativism instructs us that there are different ways of talking, not better or worse ways. Dialectical problems can be made worse by writing a language. Unlike English, Indian language writing systems tend to be phonetic and the words are spelled the way they sound. Although this means they are easier to learn to read than English, it also means that the same word in the same language can be spelled differently in different dialects. The best solution to this problem is to spell the word one way and let speakers pronounce the word according to their particular dialect. This is what is done with English; a word can be pronounced differently in different parts of the United States. In addition, people in England may not only pronounce English words differently than people in the United States, they may even use different words. For example, the English say petrol, while Americans say gasoline.

A final challenge to learning a language is that a student can be criticized and laughed at by fluent speakers for making errors in grammar and pronunciation. Such criticism can discourage students and even lead them to drop out of language classes. Even some immersion teachers have learned the language they are teaching as a second language, and their speaking ability can be criticized. One indigenous language teacher noted, "I don't speak like my grandmother, but I speak the language of my grandmother."

It is unlikely that adult learners will ever be able to pronounce the words in a new language in the same way that a child learning the language can, because of changes in their voice box (larynx) that occur during puberty. Repeated attempts to get adult learners to pronounce words correctly can discourage the learner, while ridiculing the mistakes they make in either pronunciation or grammar have the same effect. As mentioned previously, in *The Natural Approach*, comprehension should be the primary focus of language learning rather than efforts—which are probably futile with teenagers and adults—to get learners to "parrot" the language in imitation of a Native speaker.

7

Language and Reading

Although Native American students who are enrolled in bilingual programs, such as the one at Rock Point Community School described in chapter 2, have done very well in school, there is no question that fluency in speaking, reading, and writing English is essential for the success of any student in the United States and most of Canada. Teachers can believe that a student is fluent in English because they can talk to them about everyday occurrences in English; but in reality these students may not have what some experts who study language have termed school or academic English.

Language experts have divided language into two types: conversational English and academic/school English. *Conversational language* is the everyday language we use to talk face-to-face with our friends. When we are talking to our friends, we can assume that they share common experiences with us and we do not have to go into great detail. When we talk about Jim or Jane, we know that the person we are talking to knows all about Jim and Jane. In contrast to some situations in cities and suburbs where people do not know the names of their neighbors, in tribal communities everyone is related.

Academic language is the language of the classroom and books. The teacher may not know us and most likely we have never met the author of a book we are reading. In fact, the author may have died hundreds of years ago. When we do not share common experiences with the person we are talking to or with the author of a book, it is necessary for us to have more information on what is being said or written about. We cannot simply say "Jim" and assume our listeners or readers know who we are talking about. We must describe Jim at some length if we want our audience to know who we are talking about. This requires a different type of language.

Conversational language is developed in our homes and neighborhoods as we grow up. If our parents read bedtime stories to us and encourage us to read at home, then we also get some academic language at home; but for the most part academic language is developed in school. That is why it is sometimes also called school language.

The shift in schools from an emphasis on conversational to academic language usually comes in the third grade and leads to what has been called the "fourth-grade slump." Many minority students keep up academically with their nonminority classmates up through the third grade, but in fourth grade they start falling behind because they do not read enough to grasp the academic language that is used more and more in school after third grade.

An even larger problem for Native Americans is that they can speak a dialect of English that has been variously called Red English or Indian English. Much like Black English, or Ebonics, Indian English has some carryover in vocabulary and/or grammatical structure from one or more tribal languages, and can be considered an inferior version of English or slang. However, *linguists,* the experts who study language, consider both Indian and Black English as dialects of English that are not inferior in any way to the "standard English" that is spoken by most Americans. However, even if a dialect is not inferior, it can keep speakers from getting jobs if the interviewer cannot understand what is being said or is prejudiced. Even southern whites who speak with a "drawl" have taken classes to learn to speak standard English so that they can get jobs in New York and other northern cities.

READING

On average, Native American and many other minority students have not done as well academically as mainstream white Americans. Although many Native Americans have gone on to college and done well in school, many more have struggled. One explanation for this struggle is that they do not have full command of academic English and do not understand the meaning of many words that white Americans understand. Although everyone develops conversational English by talking

Two Types of Language

Experts who have transcribed conversations and analyzed the language and then compared the conversations to the language in books have found that conversational language tends to have one or two syllable words of Anglo-Saxon origin. Anglo-Saxon words originated with the Angles and Saxons who invaded England from Germany after the Roman Empire collapsed. In contrast, the language in textbooks after the third grade tends to be Greco-Latin in origin and longer, with more syllables. Greco-Latin words originated from the ancient Greek and Roman (Latin) languages, and before that from India (English and most other European languages are classified by linguists as Indo-European). To understand teacher lectures and textbooks, students need to widen their vocabulary beyond the Anglo-Saxon-based conversational English to the Greco-Latin-based academic language.

Charlene Jones, secretary of Connecticut's Mashantucket Pequot tribe, reads from the pages of *Fox's Soup for a Chief*, the first book written in the Pequot language. Though the Pequot language was never a written language and the last known speaker died in 1908, the tribe has reconstructed its language thanks to records made by colonists and Pequot's similarity to other Algonquian languages.

to family and friends, not everyone develops academic English. Research indicates that the main way to develop an academic English vocabulary is by reading a lot.

As indicated in chapter 3 on identity, the autobiography of Dr. Lori Arviso Alvord illustrates this need to read a lot to succeed in school. In his 1950 book, *Indian Agent*, teacher and Indian agent Albert H. Kneale recalled monotonous lessons at a boarding school where he worked in Oklahoma:

> Few of the pupils had any desire to learn to read, for there was nothing to read in their homes nor in the camp; there seemed little incentive to learn English, for there was no

opportunity to use it; there seemed to be nothing gained through knowing that "c-a-t" spells cat; arithmetic offered no attraction; not one was interested in knowing the name of the capital of New York.[67]

In his 1992 book, *Light of the Feather*, Mick Fedullo illustrates a case of cultural conflict with a student, which he heard from an Apache elder, who stated that the students' parents had

been to school in their day, and what that usually meant was a bad BIA boarding school. And all they remember about school is that there were all these Anglos trying to make them forget they were Apaches; trying to make them turn against their parents, telling them that Indian ways were evil.

Well, a lot of those kids came to believe that their teachers were the evil ones, and so anything that had to do with "education" was also evil—like books. Those kids came back to the reservation, got married, and had their own kids. And now they don't want anything to do with the white man's education. The only reason they send their kids to school is because it's the law. But they tell their kids not to take school seriously. So, to them, printed stuff is white-man stuff.[68]

Although knowing academic English does not necessarily make someone a good reader, it is the language used in most books above the third grade. To become a good reader it is helpful for preschool children to have bedtime stories read to them, have books and other reading material in their homes, and see their parents and elders reading. Research indicates that it also helps to live near a library, which is a problem for many Native American students who live on reservations. Centuries of experience with literacy in Europe, Asia, and the Middle East have made reading and writing an everyday part of cultures in those regions. Furthermore, reading is central to Christianity and Islam because of the importance of reading the Bible and the Koran. Many other religions also have sacred books for their believers to learn from.

Learning to Read by Reading Often

The U.S. Department of Education's 2000 *National Report Card on Reading* indicates that fourth graders who watched less television, read more for fun, had more reading material in their homes, and talked more about reading with family and friends are better readers. The importance a family and a culture place on literacy can make the difference as to how successful their children are in school. Young people need to learn that many movies they like to watch are based on books and that if they read these books they would find they are usually more interesting than the movie. Good examples of this are the Lord of the Rings and Harry Potter books. Children who read all the Harry Potter books or the three Lord of the Rings books have taken a step toward getting the practice they need to become fluent readers with large vocabularies—and good readers usually do well in school. Reading has some similarities to excelling in sports. While coaching (teaching) helps you learn to play the game, it is practice that makes you a good player or reader.[69]

In the Navajo Nation and some other Indian nations I am familiar with, I have seen high school gymnasiums that a college or university would be proud to have on its campus, but I have never seen one of these schools with a library that a college or university would be proud to have on its campus. Teachers often have to spend their own money if they want to provide additional books for their students; while on the other hand, coaches do not have to pay for their players' athletic equipment. Valedictorian students from schools that emphasize athletics over academics, in some cases, have gone to community colleges and found the work too difficult.

As mentioned previously, some Native Americans have

negative attitudes toward literacy because of its association with European "conquerors," past repressive U.S. Bureau of Indian Affairs (BIA) boarding schools, and Christian missionary efforts. Native people who share this view see literacy as taking them away from their indigenous oral culture and assimilating them into white society. However, it is a mistake to identify literacy exclusively with Europeans or Christians, as Mayans, Arabs, and Asians can point out. In addition, students who learn to read in their Native language can use these habits and skills to learn to read English or some other language.

In their book *Collected Wisdom*, Linda Cleary and Thomas Peacock reported how some Native American students exhibit resistance to reading and writing because their teachers continually correct them. They also experience comprehension problems that result from being unfamiliar with English idioms and dialects, as well as classroom instruction that does not relate well to the world they live in. However, there are many excellent books by and about Native Americans that students can read.

The Reading Wars: Phonics versus Whole Language

There is an educational and political battle going on between those who support an emphasis on phonics versus those who favor an emphasis on whole language. This battle is being waged in newspaper editorial pages, in state legislatures, and Congress. Proponents of *phonics* (the sounding out of words) point to falling reading test scores, which they see as a result of whole language instruction and scientific studies that in turn indicate phonics instruction produces better reading test scores than other methods. The supporters of *whole language* emphasize reading to children and getting children to understand what they read. They point to the fact that many English words do not follow phonetic rules and that students who simply sound out words are parroting. Whole language advocates point to other reasons to explain instances of falling reading scores, like children watching more and more television, and to the importance of actually observing children as they try to read to understand what needs to be done to help them.

As education moved from the home into schools in the nineteenth century, textbooks were developed to teach reading. The McGuffey Readers were among the first of these. They consisted of a graded series of books that are called basal readers. The first-and second-grade books were specially written to include stories that emphasized the sounds of letters in the words, but the readers for older students were anthologies of stories drawn from a variety of sources. In addition to helping teach reading, the McGuffey Readers emphasized values like rich people helping the poor and being kind to animals. Instruction in the nineteenth century tended to be teacher-centered with students doing a lot of memorization.

In the early twentieth century, the Progressive Education movement, led by philosopher and educator John Dewey, called for instruction that focused more on the interests of students and what science was discovering about teaching and learning. More and more stories were included in reading textbooks that emphasized particular sounds or targeted specific reading skills. These specially written stories with controlled vocabularies were often of little interest to students and did not include ethnic minority characters. In the 1950s, the very popular Dick and Jane readers were "all white" and used a "whole word" approach to teach reading. Words were repeated on each page enough times so that, according to behaviorist research, students could remember them. For instance, a passage would read: "See Spot run, run Spot run," with Spot being Dick and Jane's pet dog.

Phonics proponents, led by Rudolf Flesch, who, in his 1955 book *Why Johnny Can't Read*, attacked the whole word approach because it did not support the use of children's stories that did not have carefully controlled vocabularies in which words were repeated, as in the Dick and Jane readers. Phonics advocates focused their efforts on the primary grades and emphasized the importance of students having phonemic awareness—an understanding of the alphabetic principle that the spelling of words relates to how they sound when spoken. A problem with English is that it does not have a one-to-one sound symbol relationship that makes reading easier. The homonyms (words that sound the same but are spelled differently) in English, such as *to*, *too*, and *two* and *there*, *their*, and *they're*, make spelling difficult for students, even at the college level.

Although knowing basic phonetic rules helps students sound out words, other very common "outlaw words" in English still need to be memorized as sight words because they do not follow any but the most complicated rules. Other problems with phonics include the varying size of students' vocabularies and different dialects of English, which pronounce the same word differently.

Phonics is considered a "bottom up" approach in which students "decode" meaning. The advantage of phonics is that once students get the basics down, they can go to the library and read a wide variety of children's books. This is especially true for students who come to schools with large English vocabularies.

Whole language is a controversial approach to teaching reading; one that is based on observing students learning to read and using modern theories about how students learn. With whole language, teachers are expected to provide a classroom with a lot of interesting reading material at many different reading levels and to combine speaking, listening, reading, and writing. Whole language teachers emphasize the meaning of texts over the sounds of letters, and phonics instruction becomes just one component of the whole language classroom.

Whole language is considered a "top down" approach in which the reader constructs a personal meaning about what they are reading based on what they already know. The primary drawback to the whole language approach is the lack of structure; instructors don't use the teacher guides that come with textbooks.

Behaviorism versus Constructivism

Various approaches to reading presume that students learn differently. The phonics emphasis in reading draws heavily from behaviorist learning theory that is associated with the work of

Dick and Jane's Effect on a Pueblo Indian

Books used in Indian schools during the 1960s and in preceding decades usually reflected an all-white middle-class culture that had no relation to Native American life. University of New Mexico Professor Dr. Joseph H. Suina from Cochiti Pueblo described how reading Dick and Jane affected him:

The Dick and Jane reading series in the primary grades presented me with pictures of a home with a pitched roof, straight walls, and sidewalks. I could not identify with these from my Pueblo world. However, it was clear I didn't have these things and what I did have did not measure up. At night, long after grandmother went to sleep, I would lay awake staring at our crooked adobe walls casting uneven shadows from the light of the fireplace. The walls were no longer just right for me. My life was no longer just right. I was ashamed of being who I was and I wanted to change right then and there. Somehow it became so important to have straight walls, clean hair and teeth, and a spotted dog to chase after. I even became critical and hateful toward my bony, fleabag of a dog. I loved the familiar and cozy surroundings of my grandmother's house but now I imagined it could be a heck of a lot better if only I had a white man's house with a bed, a nice couch, and a clock. In school books, all the child characters ever did was run around chasing their dog or a kite. They were always happy . . ."*

* Joseph. H. Suina, "When I Went to School," in *Linguistic and Cultural Influences on Learning Mathematics*, eds. Rodney Cocking and Jose P. Mestre (Hillsdale, N.J.: Lawrence Erlbaum, 1988), 298.

Harvard psychologist B.F. Skinner. The whole language approach, on the other hand, draws from constructivist learning theory and the work of the Russian psychologist Lev Vygotsky.

Behaviorist learning theory is based on studies of animal behaviors in which animals like pigeons learned to do tasks when they received rewards and stopped doing tasks when they were not rewarded or were punished. Most of us can point to things we continue to do because we are rewarded for doing them. Rewards can be the pay we get for jobs we do, desired recognition like "A" grades, and praise from our friends. Likewise, we can point to things we stopped doing because we were not rewarded or were punished for them. Behaviorist learning theory tends to look at extrinsic, or external, rewards like money, grades, and gold stars, rather than intrinsic rewards like feeling good about successfully accomplishing a difficult task.

Constructivist learning theory is based on the idea that children learn by connecting new knowledge to previously learned knowledge. If children cannot relate new knowledge to what they already know in a meaningful way, they may memorize it, but they will not have a real understanding of what they are learning. Vygotsky identified a "zone of proximal" development in which children can learn new things that are a little

Learning Theories Compared	
Behaviorism	**Constructivism**
Teacher-Centered Direct Instruction	Student-Centered Instruction
Transmission Method	Experiential-Interactive Method
Phonics Emphasis	Whole Language Emphasis
Sound and Skills Emphasis	Meaning Emphasis

above their current understanding, with the help of more knowledgeable peers or adults. This new knowledge then becomes part of what they know.

Students who come from "high literacy" households—in which young children are read bedtime stories on a regular basis, there are many children's books, and adults read regularly—tend to learn to read well regardless of the teaching approach used. These students tend to enter school with large vocabularies and reading readiness skills (and sometimes they already can read).

Students from "low literacy" households are not exposed much to reading in their homes and tend to have smaller vocabularies. They may speak nonstandard dialects of English, such as Indian English, and can be unmotivated students, especially if they see teachers as enemies trying to change how they speak and act, that is, trying to change their language and culture. It has been argued that standard phonics approaches can be unsuccessful for these students. Whole language approaches encourage teachers to find reading material that reflects these students' language and culture.

Publishing basal reading textbooks is a multimillion-dollar industry that responds to the demands of purchasers. California and Texas, two states with large populations, have their own academic standards, and whatever they want in their textbooks, publishers tend to supply. Currently, publishers are including systematic phonics instruction, more classic and popular children's literature, and whole language activities. This compromise generally falls under the rubric of a "balanced approach" to teaching reading. Advocates of balanced reading instruction supplement a school's adopted reading program with materials that reflect the experiential background and interests of their students.

Oglala Sioux educator Dr. Sandra Fox writes in her 2001 curriculum, *Creating Sacred Places for Students*, that "reading to children is the single most important activity that parents can provide to help their children succeed in school." She recommends that teachers:

1) Use reading materials that relate to children's lives, to help them understand that literature is experience written down and that it is interesting to read.

2) Strengthen and expand children's language abilities by providing them many opportunities to have new experiences, to learn new words, and to practice oral language in English and in their Native language.[70]

8

Teaching and Learning Styles

DIRECT INSTRUCTION VERSUS EXPERIENTIAL-INTERACTIVE

There is an ongoing debate today—which dates back a century or more—over the best teaching method. On one side of the debate are advocates of teacher-centered direct instruction, who maintain it is the teacher's job to transmit to their students basic skills and the wisdom of the ages, usually through the use of lectures and textbooks in a process called direct instruction. On the other side of the debate are advocates of child-centered instruction in which it is the teachers' job to be a guide and facilitator to help students construct knowledge through hands-on activities such as science experiments.

In his research, Jim Cummins[71] has found that direct instruction, or the transmission method, does not work well with many children, but it is especially a problem for ethnic minority children. These children are often under pressures to assimilate and may resist their teachers' efforts, as described in chapter 3. In addition, direct instruction does not get students to think for themselves. Students tend to sit passively in their classrooms, often getting bored, which can eventually lead them to drop out of school. Educational consultant Mick Fedullo tells the story of walking through a school in San Jose, California. When he walked by a classroom where the students were sitting quietly at their desks the principal smiled, but when he walked past a classroom where the students were talking the principal frowned. Although noisy classrooms can be disruptive, they don't have to be if students are talking about what they are learning; it is by talking that students learn language. Fedullo had been hired by the school to help teachers develop their students' English language skills. However, the principal seemed more interested in discipline than learning.

Cummins' research found that students who were exposed to *experiential-interactive* teaching methods were more successful than those receiving direct instruction. Experiential refers to the educational philosopher John Dewey's idea of "learning by doing." At Rock Point Community School, students learned science by doing science experiments, and as they talked to each other about those experiences/experiments in class they learned language. This discussion between students is the "interactive" part of what Cummins' recommends.

The experiential-interactive approach to teaching and learning that Cummins describes is related to the "project method" that was used successfully with Native American students in the 1930s and 1940s. In the 1933 edition of his book, *How We Think*, John Dewey recommended that teachers engage students in "constructive occupations" or "projects" that engage students' interest, have intrinsic worth, awaken student curiosity, and are carried out over an extended period of time.[72]

Another experiential-interactive teaching method that has been used effectively with Native American students is the language experience approach to teaching reading. In this approach, the reading teacher begins by providing the students with a tangible experience. This can be a short walking field trip to collect leaves or an in-class experience as simple as making a peanut butter and jelly sandwich. The teacher talks about the activity the students are doing and asks the students to describe what they did. This description by the students is written down by the teacher on a chalkboard or chart paper and is then used to teach the students to read.

A major problem with textbooks used to teach reading is that the words in them, like the words in high-stakes tests, may have never been learned or spoken by the students. Young students on the Navajo Reservation in Arizona may have never seen an ocean or know the many words that relate to oceans, ships, and sea life. Alaskan students may not know much about hot deserts, cacti, and the like. If this is the case, especially when the teacher uses a lot of phonics, the students can pronounce the words like Luther Standing Bear described in chapter 6, but they do not understand what they are reading—they are just parroting. By allowing the students to participate in activities, they can be kept interested, and they know the words because they are using them as they talk about the activities they do with their teacher.

LEARNING STYLES

Native American students who come from a tribal culture that emphasizes a watch and learn process are generally visual learners who learn best when the teacher uses classroom instruction that includes graphs, films, demonstrations, and pictures. In contrast, most white children begin school as auditory learners who are encouraged to express ideas in the form of speech and tend to do well when the teacher lectures to them.

Native American students tend to be reflective or pause to consider options before responding rather than being impulsive and answering immediately. A reflective student tends to delay making a response until all evidence is collected. Often

Native American students spend more time watching and listening and less time talking than white students, as was the case with Dr. Lori Arviso Alvord at Dartmouth, whose experience was described in chapter 3. Although today we often ask students to learn by trial and error (experimenting), this approach has its shortcomings; whether it was young Native Americans hunting dangerous animals or young people today experimenting with illegal drugs. An approach that espouses watching, waiting, and learning from the successes and mistakes of others seems a much more intelligent way to learn.

The Native American view of the world can be at odds with white values and behaviors. Threats of physical punishment and force are often not the best methods of discipline. However, the idea that Native Americans never used physical discipline on their children is simplistic and wrong. In cultures that value courage, beating a child to make them say they are sorry makes no sense. In such a culture, the child who takes the whipping without crying is the child who is best exhibiting the culture's values.

Although the biblical idea of "spare the rod and spoil the child" can be rightly questioned, the idea that we should not spank or otherwise physically discipline children has its problems as well. Today, we tend not to spank students at home and in school as much as in the past, but when the child does something seriously wrong as a young teenager, the trend has moved to treating them more and more like an adult, sending them to an adult court, and then to an adult jail. It would seem that if children learned earlier that they would be burnt if they stuck their hand in a fire (rather than trying to keep them out of all danger) and punished if they hit another child without good cause, they would be less likely to end up in prison as teenagers and adults.

Ideally, culturally specific discipline—such as explanations to the children of what is good behavior—can work if it comes from a parent or elder. Discipline that comes from an extended family member, like an uncle, can make the parent-child relationship easier, just as having a principal handle discipline in school can insure that teachers have a better relationship with their students. Parents and teachers have to spend time with their children/students every day, and if their relationship is soured by necessary discipline, the home or classroom experience can become combative. However, when an uncle or principal carries out the discipline, they do not have to have that hour after hour contact with the child. The parent or teacher can be the "good cop," and the uncle or principal can be the "bad cop."

The family, the elders, and the tribe are all important in improving American Indian and Alaska Native schooling. The extended family often makes major contributions in raising children. Elders are highly respected and provide social acceptance and approval, though it should be remembered that not all old people have the wisdom to qualify to be elders. The tribe plays a fundamental role in creating cultural identity. Cultural values that are present in many tribes include generosity, which allows young people the freedom to make choices, and not to worry about getting somewhere and doing something at an exact time.

Teachers who want to successfully educate Native students should understand their own worldviews and how they perceive Native students' accepted ways of showing what they know. Matching teaching styles with learning styles promotes meaningful teacher-pupil relationships and helps student achievement. In their 1998 book, *Transforming the Culture of Schools: Yup'ik Eskimo Examples,* Jerry Lipka and Gerald Mohatt found that Alaska Native children were raised in their villages to be self-reliant and given a great deal of responsibility. However, in school, non-Native teachers were telling them "what to do, when to do it, and how to do it." The Alaska Native Yup'ik teachers emphasized "establishing a strong personal relationship with students," in contrast to the non-Native

American idea that "good teachers" were teachers who worked to replace Yup'ik language and traditional cultural knowledge and values.

The growing number of Yup'ik teachers was faced with confronting cultural conflicts just as their students were. In 1987, they formed a group of all the certified Yup'ik teachers, which served as a general support group and expanded over time to include village elders. Yup'ik teachers needed this support because their "culture conflicts powerfully with cherished values associated with mainstream schooling and society." In addition, "traditional cultures face a series of modern choices" and Yup'ik teachers act as cultural brokers, "negotiating a curriculum with the help of both village elders and outside facilitators," such as university professors. The "culturally negotiated curriculum" that Lipka and Mohatt found being developed offers more than a compromise and is not simply a matter of "taking the best from both cultures." It is a complex process of decision making that must go on in every community to determine what is best for that community and its children.[73]

American Indian and Alaska Native students traditionally tend to favor cooperation over competition, though this extends only to one's own team when playing a team sport like basketball or football. To the Native student, one's self-worth is ideally based on the ability and willingness to share in an environment that values harmony, unity, and a basic oneness. There is no value being above or below the status of other students in the classroom. Competition often makes American Indian and Alaska Native children feel isolated if the teacher points out their superior work to the class; sometimes this results in high achieving students not doing their best to regain their place in the group.

MOTIVATING STUDENTS

The 2002 No Child Left Behind Act promotes the idea that if students and schools are threatened with failing they will want to succeed; however, such a behaviorist rewards and punishment approach does not recognize the complexities of motivating people. Middle-class students who have strong parent support have been read to before they ever arrived at school and have parents who want them to go to college; consequently, they have a good chance at succeeding in school. However, children of parents who resented the assimilationist pressures and punishments they received in school may come to school with a "chip on their shoulder." These students need to be motivated with more than the fear of flunking or not graduating.

In his 1993 book, *Punished by Rewards*, Alfie Kohn looked at the research on student motivation and concluded that external or *extrinsic rewards*, including praise, grades, and tokens (like smelly stickers and candy for younger students or even money to reward older students for good grades) can have negative effects on students' academic performance. He concludes "don't praise people, only what people do," "make praise as specific as possible," "avoid phony praise," and "avoid praise that sets up competition."[74] Instead of using external rewards to motivate students, Kohn recommends educators should give students interesting educational material, a learning community environment, and choice. When students find what they are studying is interesting and enjoyable, they are being intrinsically rewarded for their learning.

Although Kohn only supports giving *intrinsic rewards*, other researchers argue that extrinsic and intrinsic motivation can be used together to encourage students to learn. In a cross-cultural study of indigenous students drawn from Australia, the United States, and Canada, Australian researcher Dennis McInerney supported Kohn's conclusion that extrinsic rewards are not associated with high academic achievement for indigenous students. Students with a strong sense of purpose for schooling were the ones who did well. These students understood that what they were learning in school would help them understand themselves and the world and would prepare them for adult jobs. In many cultures, including Plains Indian cultures, youth go on vision quests seeking self-knowledge and spiritual power. These young people head out alone to a mountain or to another place and fasted and prayed, seeking self-purification and a vision that will point to the seeker's true path in life. Youth today still need to seek a vision of their true path in life and work to understand the role of schooling in traveling that path.

Historically, in studies of non-Native American achievement motivation there has been a focus on individualism and the individual achievement of goals, and indigenous children worldwide have been stereotyped as lacking motivation to achieve academic success. However, beliefs about indigenous motivation in schools are often based only on teachers' opinions, which replicate stereotypes found in textbooks and old studies of Native Americans.

McInerney and Karen Swisher (Standing Rock Sioux), the president of Haskell Indian Nations University, found that for Navajo students the "level of competitiveness is not a crucial factor in determining the child's attitude to schooling and achievement" and "to the extent the children strongly agreed with the intention of completing school, they strongly disagreed with the need for recognition!" They found:

- As a group, Navajo students were highly achievement-oriented.
- Students who strove for excellence in their schoolwork were more confident.
- The desire for group leadership among Navajo students was significantly related to their confidence at school and desired occupation after leaving school.
- Social concern for other people in the school was related to how much Navajo students liked school.

Socially concerned students liked school more and expressed more interest in graduating.

McInerney and Swisher concluded that "clearly those students who set goals and see a purpose in their schooling are among the more successful students" and that "some students realize that they can work well in two cultures, that of the school and that of the home, and that in adopting strategies for school success, such as striving for excellence in one's school work and being future oriented, does not necessarily mean acculturation to broadly based white values." They emphasized the great importance of community values. Children who are told by their tribal community that it is good to do well in school and that one's opportunities are improved by doing well in school *will* do better in school. McInerney's research found that for indigenous children, parents were the major influence in keeping their children in school. In addition, the feelings students had about school and the support they saw themselves getting from teachers and friends was critical in getting them to stay in school.[75]

Navajo Professor Angela Willeto reported her study of 451 Navajo high school students in eleven different schools in 1999 in the *Journal of American Indian Education*. She found that students who participated in their traditional Navajo culture, as measured by involvement in traditional Navajo ceremonies and speaking Navajo, did as well in school as more assimilated Navajos.

McInerney also found that students who were given some control over what they did in school did better in school, and Deyhle found that students with a strong sense of identity could overcome the inequalities in American society and the discrimination they faced as Native Americans. Modern Native American students have largely adapted to school learning, but they still have some distance to go to be fully successful.

One needs to be very careful not to make generalizations

Learning about and participating in the ways of one's culture gives many Native American students an important sense of self, which can help them do better in school. Here, a seventh-grader (right) from the Paschal Sherman Indian School, on Oregon's Colville Indian Reservation, participates in a powwow at the school's annual Sunflower Festival.

about Native American students because of the tremendous variations among their living conditions; these variations include living in large cities or isolated rural settings and following either a traditional way of life or being acculturated into mainstream American society. But it seems clear that many, if not most, Native American parents believe that education in the classroom is necessary for their children to become successful. However, it is not clear that Native American parents in general have accepted that they need to be openly supportive of academics in their homes (doing things like reading to their preschool children) and that Native American educators have learned that they need to be supportive of their students' cultural identity, whether that identity is traditionally oriented or not. The No Child Left Behind Act calls for using teaching methods and curriculum in schools that are research-based. For American Indian and Alaska Native students, it is critical that this research be done on Native American students.

SELF-ESTEEM

Many teachers think they can help their students, especially minority students, by building their self-esteem. Although we certainly want students to feel good about themselves, there is a danger in promoting self-esteem. It used to be thought that juvenile detention facilities and prisons were full of people with low self-esteem. However, newer research shows that prisoners often have an exaggerated sense of self worth rather than the opposite. People who think themselves better than other people can think they have nothing left to learn from others and can be very dangerous. Bullies do not have low self-esteem. Perhaps it is stating the case too strongly, but grade inflation (giving most students very high grades), which has helped students' self-esteem in the short run, tends to catch up with them at the point when they go off to college or try to get any kind of job that requires academic preparation.

It is dangerous to emphasize the importance of self-esteem and ignore the hard work of making ourselves better people. Although high self-esteem can mean we feel good about ourselves, it can also mean that we are conceited, arrogant, and egotistical. Egocentric people do not show much concern for other people, just as ethnocentric people do not show much regard for other cultures and countries. Most Americans have inflated views of themselves: Studies show that one quarter of Americans think they are in the top 1 percent and few believe that they are below average, when in reality half of us are below average by definition.

A better goal than promoting self-esteem is promoting

self-efficacy. *Self-efficacy* is the idea that people feel good about themselves when they can do things they want to do. If a teacher helps a child learn to read, that child has gained a skill that should make him or her feel good about themselves. Self-control (including self-discipline) can also be better than self-esteem.

Good teachers tend to evaluate students based more on the effort they put into their class work and the improvement they show rather than on how they score on tests. This allows all students a chance at earning good grades. If grades are only given

What Students Want

Navajo students interviewed at Monument Valley High School in the Navajo Nation were asked, "What kind of teacher do you learn the most from?" Here were their responses:

* I learn the most from teachers who have hands-on projects. They listen to your ideas. They don't make you feel uncomfortable when you talk to them.
* Teachers that explain new ideas and show new ideas on how to learn different things in different ways.
* Ones that show respect and teach me responsibility.
* She can always help and explain things when you don't understand.
* I learn the most from strict teachers who give homework, who are easy to be with, and have a good sense of humor.

When asked, "If you were a teacher, what would you do in your classroom? What wouldn't you do?" Their replies included:

* Teach kids, be honest, and I wouldn't yell at my students. I will have to be patient.
* As a teacher, I will try to get to know each person individually. To see how they were doing at home and at school.
* Help them but never put them down, help them understand and make learning fun and interesting.

based on how well students do on tests, students who are advantaged—for instance, having computers and lots of books at home—can get good grades without working very hard, while ethnic minority students from low-income families have little chance to get good grades and can give up on school.

COMMUNITY-BASED TEACHING

At a parent conference at Tuba City High School in the Navajo Nation, my son Tsosie's high school chemistry teacher, Mansel Nelson, told me about how in his first year of teaching his best

* I will teach my class, treat them the way they want to be treated.

For the question, "What are some things that teachers do that may prevent you from learning?" Their responses included:

* Slams about their culture.
* Having boring lectures, talking too slow.
* Letting kids mess around or talk when someone else is talking.
* They move through a section of work too fast, and don't explain the work, often speak too quickly and don't repeat themselves.

In response to the question, "Do you believe effective teachers need to be aware and sensitive of the culture of the students they are teaching?" The overwhelming response was in favor of cultural sensitivity. They believed it was important so that their culture was not made fun of and so that the teacher was not put in an unknowing situation that could allow them to offend their students. However, some students expressed the fact that they still want to be taught the basic skills: "reading, math, writing, with culture not being a big issue."*

* Greg Prater, A. Rezzonico, R. Pyron, J. Chischille, V. Arthur and B. Yellowhair, "Effective Teachers: Perceptions of Native American Students in Rural Areas," in *Proceedings of the American Council on Rural Special Education*, USA, 1995, 358–361.

chemistry student asked him: "Why are we learning this?" This made him start thinking about how he could make chemistry more relevant to the lives of his students and thus motivate them better.

When I was in high school (my father was a university engineering professor), I would have answered this student's question in this manner: "So I can get into a good university." However, many of the students at Tuba City either do not think much about going to college or, if they do, do not have a very clear idea about how they need to prepare to get into college.

My son's teacher had become a teacher using the alternative certification route. He had a degree in chemistry and served as a chemist in the military for a number of years. Starting his teaching career at Tuba City, he naturally relied heavily on the chemistry textbook he inherited from a former teacher. Although the textbook assignments included hands-on chemistry activities, they failed to adequately motivate many of his students.

Experiencing the problems many high school teachers face with unmotivated students, my son's teacher started taking summer classes and going to workshops to find out if he could improve his teaching. He started learning about issues-based teaching in which students are given a chemistry-related problem to study. From there he moved on to a problem-based curriculum that looked at chemistry-related aspects of environmental and other issues facing the United States and the world. But he had his most success teaching when he focused on issues that affected the Tuba City community.

He had students research the SuperFund uranium tailings site (just to the east of Tuba City), and the quality of the local water and diabetes (a major local health problem). These community-based topics became the center of the curriculum, and the textbook became one resource that the students consulted in their research on the problem being studied. For example, when they studied diabetes, they used the nutrition section of the textbook and library resources, interviewed health professionals at the local hospital, and put together an information pamphlet in English and Navajo, which they distributed and explained to community members at the local supermarket during a community health day. Thus, his teaching methodology shifted from a textbook-centered approach to an experiential-interactive approach.

Unfortunately, other teachers complained about students missing their classes to go on field trips or work in informational booths, and this teacher, who was my son's best teacher at Tuba City, is now working at Northern Arizona University. It is interesting to note that the days these students missed because of field trips were much fewer than the days other students missed participating in athletic events; but no coaches were reprimanded or criticized in the same way as my son's teacher.

This does not mean that his students automatically did great in college chemistry. There is no one way to teach that guarantees success. There is in teaching a question of depth versus breadth. Students who work on a project can learn about a topic in depth, but they also need to learn about a lot of other topics, and some direct instruction and textbook work can help students cover a larger amount of material. The Native American idea of balance and harmony in life (avoiding the extremes) implies that teachers need to combine some direct instruction with some experiential-interactive teaching.

The type of community-based curriculum and experiential-interactive teaching methods that my son's teacher used at Tuba City to motivate and engage his students can be used at any grade level in any subject. Mainstream students who are fluent in English and read well can survive a textbook-dominated curriculum even if they do not like it, but Native Americans need more hands-on experiences, such as those my son's chemistry teacher provided, in order to understand what they are being taught.

At one extreme are modern teaching methods and materials that treat both teachers and students like robots. The teachers are told exactly what to do, and they tell the students exactly what to do. Research has supposedly "proven" that these methods and materials will work with all students. At the other extreme are teachers who would ignore what parents, school administrators, and school boards want them to teach in favor of what they believe works best. There needs to be room for compromise so teachers can be responsive to the unique needs of their students, rather than slavishly teaching from textbooks and "canned" curriculums that almost never reflect the tribal heritage of their students. These "canned" curriculums are sold to schools the way salespeople sell used cars; with promises of how great they are, but in the end not living up to the sales pitches, especially when used with Native American and other ethnic minority students.

Students in school can be torn between learning a little about a lot of things and a lot about a few things. Direct instruction through lectures and textbooks can expose students to a large breadth of material, while interactive-experiential projects can allow them to study a few subjects in depth. It is possible to combine seemingly incompatible teaching approaches, such as phonics and whole language or direct instruction and experiential-interactive instruction, into balanced approaches that draw from strengths of both extremes. The current danger of the federal government's No Child Left Behind Act for Native American students is that the high-stakes tests it mandates ignore Native American traits, especially in regard to local communities and environments, and instead focuses on the breadth of the students' learning.

It is time to remember what Luther Standing Bear declared in 1933 about young Native Americans needing to be "doubly educated" so that they learn "to appreciate both their traditional life and modern life."[76] We need to, as one indigenous teacher has commented, "Get beyond the notion you can only be smart in English."

1819 Civilization Act enacted.

1824 Indian Office established in the U.S. War Department.

1879 Carlisle Indian Industrial School founded.

1928 Meriam Report criticizes Indian education.

1934 Indian Reorganization and Johnson O'Malley Acts passed.

1947 Indian Office shifted to U.S. Department of the Interior and renamed Bureau of Indian Affairs.

1955 Institute for American Indian Studies founded at University of South Dakota.

1959 Center for Indian Education founded at Arizona State University.

1961 *Journal of American Indian Education* begins publication.

1963 Martin Luther King gives his "I Have a Dream" speech.

1966 Rough Rock Demonstration School founded.

1967 California Indian Education Association formed.

1967–1971 National Study of Indian Education carried out.

1968 Bilingual Education Act passed.

1969 National Indian Education Association founded; Navajo Community College (now Diné College) opens; *Indian Education: A National Tragedy, A National Challenge* (Kennedy Report) issued.

1969–1971 Native Americans occupy Alcatraz Island in San Francisco Bay.

1970 Haskell Institute becomes Haskell Indian Junior College.

1972 American Indian Higher Education Consortium formed; Village of Wounded Knee taken over by American Indian Movement on Pine Ridge Reservation in South Dakota; Indian Education Act passed.

1973 Rock Point Community School goes contract; Cree Way project in Quebec, Canada, started.

1975 Indian Self Determination and Education Act passed.

1978 American Indian Language Development Institute (AILDI) established.

1982 Maori preschool language nests first established.

1984 *Punana Leo* Hawaiian language preschools started; Navajo Tribal Education Policies enacted.

1985 Northern Ute Language Policy enacted.

1989 *Tribal College Journal* starts publication.

1990 Native American Languages Act passed; Indian Nations at Risk Task Force chartered by U.S. Secretary of Education.

1991 Custer Battlefield National Monument becomes Little Bighorn Battlefield, N.M.

1992 White House Conference on Indian Education held; Sinte Gleska College becomes Sinte Gleska University.

1993 Haskell Indian Junior College becomes Haskell Indian Nations University.

1996 Teacher Education Program started at Navajo Community College.

1998 President William J. Clinton's Executive Order on American Indian and Alaska Native Education.

2002 No Child Left Behind Act passed.

2004 President George W. Bush's Executive Order on American Indian and Alaska Native Education.

Notes

Chapter 1:
Assimilation and the Native American

1   Albert H. Neal, *Indian Agent* (Caldwell, Idaho: Caxton, 1950), 41.

2   John Collier, *The Indians of the Americas: The Long Hope* (New York: W.W. Norton, 1947), 17.

3   ——. *From Every Zenith: A Memoir* (Denver, Colo.: Sage Books, 1963), 203.

4   *Annual Report of the Commissioner of Indian Affairs* (Washington, D.C.: U.S. Government Printing Office, 1885), cxiii.

5   Estelle Fuchs and Robert G. Havighurst, *To Live on This Earth: American Indian Education* (Garden City, N.Y.: Anchor Books, 1972), 19, 170, 187.

6   Special Subcommittee on Indian Education, Senate Committee on Labor and Public Welfare, *Indian Education: A National Tragedy, A National Challenge* (Washington, D.C.: U.S. Government Printing Office, 1969), ix.

7   Ralph Nader, "Statement of Ralph Nader, Author, Lecturer." *Indian Education*, pt. 1, 47–55. Hearings before the Subcommittee on Indian Education of the Committee on Labor and Public Welfare. U.S. Senate, 91st Cong., 1st sess. (Washington, D.C.: U.S. Government Printing Office, 1969), 49, 51.

8   Richard Nixon, "Special Message to Congress on Indian Affairs." In *Public Papers of the Presidents of the United States, Richard Nixon. Containing the Public Messages, Speeches, and Statements of the President, 1970* (Washington, D.C.: U.S. Government Printing Office, 1971), 565.

9   George Wharton James, *What the White Race May Learn from the Indian* (Chicago, Ill.: Forbes, 1908), 25.

Chapter 2:
Community-Controlled Schools and Tribal Colleges

10 Brodrick Johnson, *Navaho Education at Rough Rock* (Rough Rock, Ariz.: Rough Rock Demonstration School, 1968), 21.

11 John Collier, Jr., "Survival at Rough Rock: A Historical Overview of Rough Rock Demonstration school," *Anthropology and Education*, vol., 19, 1988, 253.

12 Robert A. Roessel, Jr., *An Analysis of Select Navajo Needs with Implications for Navajo Education*, Ed.D., dissertation, Arizona State University, 1960, 13–14.

13 ——. "The Right To Be Wrong and the Right To Be Right," *Journal of American Indian Education* 7 (no. 2, 1968): 5.

14 Donald Erickson, *Community School at Rough Rock: A Report Submitted to the Office of Economic Opportunity*, 1969, 4, 12.

15 Gloria Emerson, "The Laughing Boy Syndrome," *School Review* 79 (1970): 94–95, 97.

16 Task Force Five: Indian Education. *Report on Indian Education: Final Report to the American Indian Policy Review Commission* (Washington, D.C.: U.S. Government Printing Office, 1976), 259.

17 Wayne Holm, "Let It Never Be Said," *Journal of American Indian Education* 4 (no. 1, 1964). Available at *http://jaie.asu.edu/v4/ V4S1let.html*

18 Hildegard Thompson, "Experience: Prerequisite to Language," *Indian Education* 28 (no. 416, 1965): 3.

19 Paul Rosier and Wayne Holm, *Bilingual Education Series: 8; The Rock Point Experience: A Longitudinal Study of a Navajo School Program (Saad Naaki Bee Na'nitin).* (Washington D.C.: Center for Applied Linguistics, 1980), vi.

20 Lewis Meriam, ed., *The Problem of Indian Administration* (Baltimore, Md.: John Hopkins University Press, 1928), 33.

21 Clyde Kluckhohn, *Culture and Behavior* (New York: The Free Press of Glencoe, 1962), 340.

22 History of the Akwesasne Freedom School. Available at *http://www.potsdam.edu/EDUC/ Akwesasn/History.html*

23 Peter MacDonald and Ted Schwarz, *The Last Warrior: Peter MacDonald and the Navajo Nation* (New York: Orion Books, 1993), 49.

24 *NCA (North Central Association) Self Study 2002* (Tsaile, Ariz.: Diné College, 2002), 25.

25 Deborah House, *Language Shift among the Navajos: Identity Politics and Cultural Continuity* (Tucson, Ariz.: University of Arizona, 2002), 38, 87.

26 Oglala Lakota College. *Oglala Lakota College Catalog 2000–2001* (Kyle, S.D.: OLC, 2001), 79.

27 Oglala Lakota College Web site: *http://www.olc.edu/*

28 Jack D. Forbes and Carolyn Johnson, eds. *Handbook for the Development of Native American Studies* (Davis, Calif.: Native American Studies, University of California–Davis, 1971), 29.

Chapter 3:
Native American Identity

29 Vine Deloria, Jr. and Daniel R. Wildcat. *Power and Place: Indian Education in America* (Golden, Colo.: Fulcrum, 2001), 71.

30 Amy Bergstrom, Linda M. Cleary, and Thomas D. Peacock, *The Seventh Generation: Native Students Speak about Finding the Good Path* (Charleston, W.Va.: ERIC Clearinghouse on Rural Education and Small Schools, 2003), 26.

31 Jim Cummins, *Language, Power and Pedagogy: Bilingual Children in the Crossfire* (Clevedon, U.K.: Multilingual Matters, 2000), 246.

32 John U. Ogbu, "Understanding Cultural Diversity and Learning." In *Handbook of Research on Multicultural Education*, eds. J.A. Banks and C.A.M. Banks (New York: Macmillan, 1995), 590.

33 Donna Deyhle, "Constructing Failure and Maintaining Cultural Identity: Navajo and Ute School Leavers." *Journal of American Indian Education*, vol. 31, no. 2, 1992, 24. Available at *http://jaie.asu.edu/v31/V31S2con.htm*

34 Ibid., 24–25.

35 Jon Reyhner, "American Indian School Dropouts and Pushouts." Available at *http://jan.ucc.nau.edu/~jar/AIE/Dropouts.html*

36 John U. Ogbu, *Black American Students in an Affluent Suburb: A Study of Academic Disengagement* (Mawah, N.J.: Lawrence Erlbaum, 2003), 148, 157, 164, 209, 213, 236.

37 Alan Peshkin, *Places of Memory: Whiteman's Schools and Native American Communities* (Hillsdale, N.J.: Lawrence Erlbaum, 1997), 5.

38 Ibid., 107, 117.

39 Ibid., 117.

40 Information is adapted from Lori Arviso Alvord, *The Scalpel and the Silver Bear* (New York: Bantam, 1999), 9.

41 Ibid., 25–26.

42 Ibid., 30.

43 Ibid., 9.

44 Ibid., 30.

45 Ibid., 50.

46 Ibid., 86.

47 Ibid., 100.

48 Ibid., 88.

Chapter 4:
Language and Culture Revitalization

49 Much of the information on the Maori, Hawaiian, Hualapai and Cree language revitalization efforts included below is adapted from Dawn B. Stiles, "Four Successful Indigenous Language Programs," in *Teaching Indigenous Languages*, ed. Jon Reyhner (Flagstaff, Ariz.: Northern Arizona University, 1997), 248–262. Accessed October 14, 2004 at *http://jan.ucc.nau.edu/~jar/TIL_21.html*

50 Mission Statement of the *Aha Pūnana Leo*. Available at *http://www.ahapunanaleo.org/MU.htm*

Chapter 5:
Language Policies and Education Goals

51 Navajo Division of Education. Navajo Nation: Educational Policies (Window Rock, Ariz.: Author, 1985), 9.

52 Northern Ute Tribe, "Ute Language Policy." *Cultural Survival Quarterly*, vol. 9, no. 2, 1985, 16.

53 *Native American Languages Act*, Public Law 101-477 (October 30, 1990).

54 Indian Nations at Risk Task Force, *Indian Nations at Risk: An Educational Strategy for Action (Final Report of the Indian Nations at Risk Task Force* (Washington, D.C.: U.S. Department of Education), iv.

55 Ibid.

56 Ibid., 20.

57 *Report for the White House Conference on Indian Education, New Mexico* (Santa Fe, N.M.: New Mexico Indian Education Association, 1991), ii.

58 Ibid., 58.

59 United States General Accounting Office, BIA and DOD Schools: Student Achievement and Other Characteristics Often Differ from Public Schools, 2001. Available at *http://www.gao.gov/new.items/d01934.pdf*.

60 *No Child Left Behind Act of 2001*, Public Law 107–110, Sec. 7101 (January 8, 2002).

Chapter 6:
Language Teaching

61 Don Talayesva, *Sun Chief: The Autobiography of a Hopi Indian*, ed. Leo W. Simmons (New Haven, Conn.: Yale University, 1942), 90.

62 Helen Sekaquaptewa, *My and Mine: The Life Story of Helen Sekaquaptewa*, as told to Louise Udall (Tucson, Ariz.: University of Arizona, 1969), 12–13.

63 John Fire, *Lame Deer: Seeker of Visions* (New York: Simon & Schuster, 1972), 23–24.

64 Luther Standing Bear, *My People the Sioux*, ed. E. A. Brininstool (Boston, Mass.: Houghton Mifflin, 1928), 239.

65 Fire, Lame Deer, 33.

66 Darell Kipp, *Encouragement, Guidance, Insights and Lessons Learned from Native Language Activists Developing Their Own Tribal Language Programs* (St. Paul, Minn.: Grotto Foundation). Available at *http://www.grotto-foundation.org/peigan.pdf*

Chapter 7:
Language and Reading

67 Albert H. Kneale, *Indian Agent* (Caldwell, Idaho: Caxton, 1950), 52–53.

68 Mick Fedullo, *Light of the Feather* (New York: Morrow, 1992), 117.

69 National Center for Education Statistics, *National Report Card on Reading 2000*. Washington, D.C.: U.S. Department of Education, 2001. Accessed February 28, 2004 at *http://nces.ed.gov/nationsreportcard/pdf/main2000/2001499.pdf*

70 Sandra J. Fox, *Creating a Sacred Place to Support Young American Indian and Other Learners* (vol. 1) (Polson, Mont.: National Indian School Board Association, 2000), 1, 3.

Chapter 8:
Teaching and Learning Styles

71 Jim Cummins, *Language, Power, and Pedagogy: Bilingual Children in the Crossfire* (Clevedon, U.K.: Multilingual Matters, 2000).

72 John Dewey, *How We Think* (revised & expanded edition) (Boston, Mass.: Houghton Mifflin, 1933), 218–219.

73 Jerry Lipka, G. Mohatt, and the Ciulistet Group, *Transforming the Culture of Schools: Yup'ik Eskimo Examples* (Mahwah, N.J.: Lawrence Erlbaum, 1998), 5, 26–27, 95, 101.

74 Alfie Kohn, *Punished by Rewards* (Boston, Mass.: Houghton Mifflin, 1993), 108–110.

75 Dennis M. McInerney and Karen G. Swisher, "Exploring Navajo Motivation in School Settings," *Journal of American Indian Education*, vol. 34, no. 3, 1995, 44. Available at *http://jaie.asu.edu/v34/V34S3exp.htm*

76 Luther Standing Bear, *Land of the Spotted Eagle* (Boston, Mass.: Houghton Mifflin, 1933), 252.

Alvord, Lori Arviso. *The Scalpel and the Silver Bear*. New York: Bantam, 1999.

Collier, John. *The Indians of the Americas: The Long Hope*. New York: W.W. Norton, 1947.

———. *From Every Zenith: A Memoir*. Denver, Colo.: Sage Books, 1963.

Cummings, Jim. *Language, Power, and Pedagogy: Bilingual Children in the Crossfire*. Clevedon, U.K.: Multilingual Matters, 2000.

Deloria, Vine, Jr., and Daniel R. Wildcat. *Power and Place: Indian Education in America*. Golden, Colo.: Fulcrum, 2001.

Fire, John. *Lame Deer: Seeker of Visions*. New York: Simon & Schuster, 1972.

Fuchs, Estelle, and Robert G. Havighurst. *To Live on This Earth: American Indian Education*. Garden City, N.Y.: Anchor Books, 1972.

House, Deborah. *Language Shift among the Navajos: Identity Politics and Cultural Continuity*. Tucson, Ariz.: University of Arizona Press, 2002.

James, George Wharton. *What the White Race May Learn from the Indian*. Chicago, Ill.: Forbes, 1908.

Kneale, Albert H. *Indian Agent*. Caldwell, Idaho: Caxton, 1950.

MacDonald, Peter, and Ted Schwarz. *The Last Warrior: Peter MacDonald and the Navajo Nation*. New York: Orion Books, 1993.

Meriam, Lewis, ed. *The Problem of Indian Administration*. Baltimore, Md.: John Hopkins University, 1982.

Peshkin, Alan. *Places of Memory: Whiteman's Schools and Native American Communities*. Hillsdale, N.J.: Lawrence Erlbaum, 1997.

Platero, Dillon. "Bilingual Education in the Navajo Nation," In *Proceedings of the First Inter-American Conference on Bilingual Education*, edited by Rudolph C. Troike and Nancy Modiano. Arlington, Va.: Center for Applied Linguistics, 1975.

Sekaquaptewa, Helen. *My and Mine: The Life Story of Helen Sekaquaptewa*, as told to Louise Udall. Tucson, Ariz.: University of Arizona Press, 1969.

Talayesva, Don. *Sun Chief: The Autobiography of a Hopi Indian*, edited by Leo W. Simmons. New Haven, Conn.: Yale University Press, 1942.

Further Reading

Books

Bergstrom, Amy, Linda Miller Cleary, and Thomas D. Peacock. *The Seventh Generation: Native Students Speak about Finding the Good Path.* Charleston, W.Va.: ERIC Clearinghouse on Rural Education and Small Schools, 2003.

Bigelow, Bill, and Bob Peterson, eds. *Rethinking Columbus: The Next 500 Years.* Milwaukee, Wisc.: Rethinking Schools, 1991.

Cajete, Gregory. *Look to the Mountain: An Ecology of Indigenous Education.* Durango, Colo.: Kivaki Press, 1994.

Cantoni, Gina, ed. *Stabilizing Indigenous Languages.* Flagstaff, Ariz.: Northern Arizona University, 1996. Retrievable at *http://www.ncela.gwu.edu/miscpubs/stabilize/index.htm*

Cleary, Linda Miller, and Thomas D. Peacock. *Collected Wisdom: American Indian Education.* Boston, Mass.: Allyn & Bacon, 1998.

Deloria, Vine, Jr. and Daniel R. Wildcat. *Power and Place: Indian Education in America.* Golden, Colo.: Fulcrum Resources, 2001.

Fuchs, Estelle, and Robert J. Havighurst. *To Live on This Earth: American Indian Education.* Albuquerque, N.M.: University of New Mexico Press, 1972.

Gilliland, Hap. *Teaching the Native American.* 4th ed. Dubuque, Iowa.: Kendall Hunt, 1999.

Indian Education: A National Tragedy, A National Challenge (The Kennedy Report). November 1969, Washington, D.C.: U.S. Government Printing Office.

Kawagley, Oscar A. *A Yupiaq Worldview: A Pathway to Ecology and Spirit.* Prospect Heights, Ill.: Waveland Press, 1995.

Reyhner, Jon, and Jeanne Eder. *American Indian Education: A History.* Norman, Okla.: University of Oklahoma Press, 2004.

———, ed. *Teaching American Indian Students.* Norman, Okla.: University of Oklahoma Press, 1992.

Slapin, Beverly, and Doris Seale, eds. *Through Indian Eyes: The Native Experience in Books for Children.* 3rd ed. Gabriola Island, B.C., Canada: New Society Publishers, 1991.

Videotapes

E Ola Ka 'Olelo Hawai'i. (1997). 'Aha Punana Leo (P.O. Box 1265 Kea'au, HI 96749). Describes the most successful effort for indigenous language revitalization in the United States. It tells the story of more than a century of decline for the Hawaiian language and the revival of its use in the past two decades. Through interviews, archival footage, and visits to Hawaiian language-immersion classrooms, this video makes a powerful statement about the value of the Hawaiian language and culture for Native Hawaiians.

Websites

American Indian Science and Engineering Society (AISES)
http://www.aises.org/

The Problem of Indian Administration (1928 Meriam Report)
http://www.alaskool.org/native_ed/research_reports/IndianAdmin/Indian_Admin_Problms.html

Teaching Indigenous Languages
http://jan.ucc.nau.edu/~jar/TIL.html

Teaching and Learning with Native Americans
http://literacynet.org/lp/namericans/contents.html

A Native Perspective on School Reform
http://www.nwrac.org/pub/hot/native.html

Society for Advancement of Chicanos and Native Americans in Science (SACNAS)
http://www.sacnas.org/

Indian Education: A National Tragedy—A National Challenge (Kennedy Report)
http://www.tedna.org/pubs/Kennedy/toc.htm

White House Conference on Indian Education (Executive Summary)
http://www.tedna.org/pubs/1990whthsconf.pdf

Index

Index

Jon Allan Reyhner, Ed.D., is Professor of Education at Northern Arizona University and has edited several books on Native American education, including *Nurturing Native Languages* (2003) and *Revitalizing Indigenous Languages* (1999). He is also coauthor of *American Indian Education: A History* (2004) and *Language and Literacy Teaching for Indigenous Education: A Bilingual Approach* (2002). Reyhner previously taught junior high school in the Navajo Nation, was a school administrator for ten years in Indian schools in Arizona, Montana, and New Mexico, and served as an assistant professor and coordinator of the Indian Bilingual Teacher Training Program.

Paul C. Rosier received his Ph.D. in American History from the University of Rochester, with a specialty in Native American History. His first book, *Rebirth of the Blackfeet Nation, 1912–1954*, was published by the University of Nebraska Press in 2001. In November 2003, Greenwood Press published *Native American Issues* as part of its Contemporary American Ethnic Issues series. Dr. Rosier has also published articles on Native American topics in the *American Indian Culture and Research Journal*, and the *Journal of American Ethnic History*. In addition, he was a coeditor of *The American Years: A Chronology of United States History*. He is Assistant Professor of History at Villanova University, where he also serves as a faculty advisor to the Villanova Native American Student Association.

Walter Echo-Hawk is a member of the Pawnee tribe. He is a staff attorney of the Native American Rights Fund (*www.narf.org*) and a Justice on the Supreme Court of the Pawnee Nation (*www.pawneenation.org/pawnee%20court/.htm*). He has handled cases and legislation affecting Native American rights in areas such as religious freedom, education, water rights, fishing rights, grave protection, and tribal repatriation of Native dead.